THROUGH THE MIND'S EYE

A Journey of Self-Discovery

J.P. WILLSON

◆ FriesenPress

Suite 300 - 990 Fort St
Victoria, BC, V8V 3K2
Canada

www.friesenpress.com

Copyright © 2016 by J.P. Willson
First Edition — 2016

All rights reserved.

No part of this publication may be reproduced in any form, or by any means, electronic or mechanical, including photocopying, recording, or any information browsing, storage, or retrieval system, without permission in writing from FriesenPress.

ISBN
978-1-4602-9251-8 (Hardcover)
978-1-4602-9252-5 (Paperback)
978-1-4602-9253-2 (eBook)

1. BISAC *code 001*

Distributed to the trade by The Ingram Book Company

Table of Contents

v	Acknowledgements
vii	Preface
1	Introduction
7	The Origins of Addiction
19	Chapter 1 *The Dry Drunk*
29	Chapter 2 *The Next Step*
39	Chapter 3 *Discovery*
49	Chapter 4 *Depression*
59	Chapter 5 *Perception*

71	Chapter 6 *Into the Great Beyond*
83	Chapter 7 *The Twelve Steps (and Then Some)*
101	Chapter 8 *Realizations*
111	Chapter 9 *And How the Mighty Have Fallen*
125	Chapter 10 *Alternatives, Options, and Other Avenues*
137	Chapter 11 *I Should Have . . .*
147	Chapter 12 *Days of Wine and Roses*
159	Bibliography
161	Resources
163	About The Author

Acknowledgements

THERE ARE a great many people that I need to thank here—so many, in fact, that I do not believe I could honestly remember them all. What I can say is that I hold a great gratitude for the staff of the Salvation Army Harbour Light addictions treatment facility in the downtown eastside of Vancouver, British Columbia. Every single person within its doors—from the treatment manager right on down the line—helped me in my recovery in their own way. Without a doubt, they are incredibly special people, and I owe them my gratitude, tenfold.

I would like to specifically mention three indelibly unique women at this centre that have a very special place in my heart: Janina, Sara, and Zahra. I have met an incredible amount of people throughout my life (more so than most), yet the true inner beauty these three exceptional women possess was, for me, an experience I will not forget. They are doing what they love; I cannot put into words how deep my feelings run. They showed me the ways in which I could learn to heal myself, how I could begin this incredible journey which is my life. I will never be able to thank them enough for the help they have given me, yet I know no thanks are needed—this is who they are, and who they shall continue to be for every life they touch. Nothing else needs be said.

These three women were my greatest inspirations for this book. My hope is that the knowledge I have learned and the experiences I have lived will help others who are suffering to come to an awakening, as I have.

Preface

As strange as this may seem, I have to admit right from the get-go that I have never written a book before. Yes, this was all very new to me, and upon the realization of what a "preface" actually was, the true meaning and the reasoning behind it did make a fair amount of sense.

According to my editor, the preface should provide a quick description of what the book is about, as well as the manner in which the author (that being me) became inspired to write said book. In addition, the preface should include a definitive account of the writing process. So I thought to myself, *I could do that; this really does make a fair amount of sense to me.*

I gave it a shot, the following is the end product of that endeavour.

This being a book about *addiction*, I felt the very best place to start was there. I have been an alcoholic for the majority of my adult life. The problem with this was that I was unable to admit this to myself, unable to face the truth. It got to the point when I was left with no other choice: I sobered up or died. When I first decided to enter the treatment program (I will go into greater detail about this later) I was unaware of how very close to death I truly was; I just wanted to stop, I did not wish to live my life any longer, just surviving day-to-day in the hopes of being able to feed my addiction. That was all I knew in the end stages of this affliction; I had to work to earn enough to be able to buy a bottle so I could forget all of my troubles for another day, only to wake up and repeat the process over again. And so it went. I had had enough of the pain and misery that defined my life. It needed to stop.

Originally, when I started the treatment program, I had no intention of writing a book; if I had, I honestly believe that I would have had my head examined. Why would *anyone* subject themselves to twenty-five years of addiction for the sole purpose of penning a book? As the program progressed, I was required to keep a daily journal of my thought processes throughout the recovery. Gradually, the significance and intrinsic therapeutic value of this journaling dawned on me. I have always enjoyed writing, simply for the sake of writing, I like to think I am an imaginative person, and I have always written for most of my life. Whether it was poetry or short stories or just plain work-related journaling, writing has been a part of my daily thought process for most of my adult life.

Throughout the program I found that not only was I helping myself to heal, but also I was able to help *others* on their own journeys. Once my head became clear enough to understand what it was that I was experiencing, I unknowingly was helping my group mates with their own processes at the same time. My journaling became so much more than just the day-to-day things I was dealing with (which, in itself, was truly monumental–I kid you not). Two pages a day somehow turned into ten, and sometimes more; whatever day it was, and whatever issues were involved, I wrote about it all. The events that occurred throughout the fourteen months I spent in the recovery program were so much more than I could ever have imagined. I wanted—and I *needed*—to have a substantial record of the entire experience. This book is just that, and I have appropriately included in the title that it is "my journey."

My primary counsellor was, unknowingly, the initial inspiration for this book. We tossed the idea back and forth between us jokingly many times during our sessions. She still has no idea that I have done this—yet she will find out soon enough.

I believe the real inspiration came from another woman that I met during the program while I was initially just trying to complete my Grade 12 Dogwood Diploma. All it took was me being asked to write a piece for the centre's newsletter, which I received positive feedback for. One thing led to another, and I re-discovered the personal power of the spoken and written word. I felt I could help others through their own deep and complex situations, which I was also dealing with. It just felt like this was something that I desperately needed to accomplish. Not surprisingly, these women—the counsellor, the woman in my program, and one more who is acknowledged throughout this book—were extraordinary in their kindness and support throughout my journey.

Introduction

OVER THE many years of my addiction, many people asked me this very pointed question: "Why is it that you don't just quit?" I had many different and varying answers to this, none of which make the slightest bit of sense to me now, with one sole exception: I realize that none of my answers were in fact answers at all; they were merely excuses, and very poor ones at that. I wonder if anyone recognizes this as a pattern. I sure didn't, at the time.

The answer that I preferred the most, simply because it was interchangeable for varying situations, was this: "I don't have a problem, I just like to drink. Really, I stop all the time, so it's not an issue." It's funny to me now that the reason I was being asked was because people were genuinely concerned about my well-being. However, because I wasn't realizing that I had an issue—or willing or able to even admit it—every time people asked, it went in one ear and out the other. There were so many years of such ignorance on my part. As I started to realize that *yes, I actually have a very serious problem*, this was the first step towards recovery. However, actually doing something about the whole situation was much more difficult for me to wrap my head around.

For the longest time I assured myself that if I just stopped drinking everything would just get better, life would be wonderful again, and people would ultimately (and this was the biggest part of my denial process) stop nagging me about all of this "trivial" nonsense. And they did—but not for the right reasons at all. Others could see that I wasn't drinking any longer, but in doing this I became a very unpleasant person to be around. I was angry and extremely moody most of the time, and the depression—which I had been unaware of as an issue—came to the forefront in my life. My job started to suffer and I began to isolate myself. I did not wish to be around others unless I specifically *had* to be.

In essence, what I am about to do in this book is show you the process that I undertook to try to understand what in the hell it was that made me an addict to begin with. *Why* am I an addict? Is there any real reason? Am I a unique individual in this respect? Of course, the answer to all of those questions is a solemn "no." Some are absolutely predisposed to the entire addiction affliction, but is there an actual reason for such? Not so much. I have spent my life with this thing that for all intents and purposes can be (and is) a truly debilitating condition—or disease, as some medical professionals have stated. Did I do something to bring this on? I often wonder about that, and in all of my now-infinite wisdom I don't think I did, yet as the whole scenario progressed over the years, I certainly did feed the addiction with my ignorance.

Knowing as much about the subject as I do helps to explain how I got to the point where I now find myself. However, my biggest question is still this: having been in recovery for such a long time—and knowing all the information about the whole addiction fiasco for the majority of my adult life—how is it that this entire thing came to fruition? What could I or anyone else have possibly done to avoid this sordid affair?

Of course, in my opinion, the answer to that is absolutely nothing. As far as it seems, for myself or anyone else, *there is no real reason*; there is no singular scientific explanation for the unfortunate circumstance of addiction. I seem to be at a point (in my somewhat skewed view) where addiction is a form of personality disorder. That being said, this is only my opinion, of which there are many throughout this book. The amount of underlying circumstances and factors leading to addiction are astronomical and sometimes extreme in their inference. These I shall explore from my standpoint, yet I am not of a one-thinking mind. My beliefs and my opinions are not solely mine, and you may or may not agree with them, but that is not the point of this; they are ideas meant to open one's mind to another's experience of addiction and the resulting recovery process, and nothing else.

There's one thing I feel I need to point out right from the start: some may find this book, these passages, condescending in nature. This is by no means my intent or my desire. I am aware of this, and I have done everything within the editing process to ensure I am in fact not doing this, yet I have no control over outside perspectives on the topic at hand and the content herein. This is a delicate subject, and there is no way I can be certain of how everyone shall use, decipher, interpret, or even generalize my opinions. Please remember while reading this that these are solely my experiences and my opinions, and that my intent is to try and help others with the knowledge I have gained throughout my recovery process. You may also find that I repeat this many times throughout my writings, and your perspective will differ from mine, I am certain of this; Chapter 5 is completely about perception.

Because I have this indescribable need to know *why* and *how* everything happens in the way that it does, I persist and succeed in finding an explanation for that which I am seeking. In the resulting writings I hope to accomplish just that, and I hope I can answer some of the questions others may have through my own experiences with addiction and recovery. I may just manage to confuse some and frustrate them further, but this is not my intention; originally, this book was to satiate my own mind, and my own skewed sense of thinking (as I referred to it earlier) was the original reason for penning this. Most of my conclusions have only opened doors to so many more queries in my mind. My hope is that this book does not have the same confusing impact on others, but instead it provides the answers they are looking for.

Through some of these writings I delve into the vast amount of insight I have gained about myself, which I truly believe could be of great help to many people. I know that to begin with, the entire process of just *writing* some of these passages was of great therapeutic value. Initially, writing helped me when I could not find someone to discuss my issues with, or when I just plain didn't want to. Mostly it was me just trying to figure out for myself what had brought me to my longstanding addiction in the first place. This was fruitless, for lack of a better word.

I will touch on depression, loneliness, frustration, anger, emotions both good and bad—anything and everything, really—that helped me to better understand my addiction and give me some sense of reason. Now, my goal is that my story—the things I have learned, and the things that I have become so acutely aware of—can be of help and use for others going through the same ordeal in their lives, to support them along their own difficult "journeys."

The Origins of Addiction

IN THE early stages of my recovery, I wondered incessantly where the addiction first manifested itself. I believe this to be one of my continuing addictions—that is, my uncontrollable urge to know the purpose of everything, how things work and why. This could be something as ridiculous as when someone mixes vinegar with baking soda in a sealed environment; why does it explode? I need to know *why* in these situations, whereas other people may say, "that was way cool," and be done with it. (Just as a forewarning, the phrase "the uncontrollable urge to know" will be repeated many times throughout these pages, so be prepared for that.)

"Addiction" as a word sounds painful, doesn't it? Ominous, even. To me, it has so many meanings that I can relate to at so many points in my life, starting from a very young age. Of course, no one knows this when they are young, simply because these are just habits to begin with. When those habits grow to the point of absolute obsession, I believe this to be an accurate description of the word "addiction."

However, a person can be obsessed with something and not have it become an addiction. For instance, cooking for me is an obsession, not an addiction. I just love to cook. Having said that, when I drank I drank because I loved the drink, nothing more; I loved the way it made me feel. When it got to the point where this was no longer the case, I stopped.

Sounds simple, right? Enough said about that; now, let's get on with our lives, let's focus on validating our little, unimportant reasons for our futile existence on this planet, which is itself a tiny speck compared to the vast, innumerable galaxies and universes that have yet to be discovered...

Was that too much? I was making a point, the point being there is no "quick fix" for the "addiction," and there never will be. Once "blessed" with this ungodly disorder, staying clean and sober for the rest of one's natural life can become an addiction in itself.

I was reading this article recently that was trying to uncover the root cause of addiction, according to this particular author. At the same time, he was also bastardizing what some research has led us to believe is the main reason for addiction: that it's the drug *itself* that gets us hooked and holds us there (hence the reason the entire "war on drugs" originated). There's this political belief that if you eradicate the origin of the drug, then there will in turn be no more addiction. When I first read this article, the only thing that came to my mind was an emphatic "no."

Then the author explained how other research shows that addiction is only related to a person's circumstance or environment. This suggests that if, in fact, you take an addict out of the environment where the addiction is occurring and place them in a drug-free set of circumstances then two things happen:

1. that person will no longer have the need to use, and

2. their life will change for the better.

Again, this is simple, right?

Every person, at one time or another, has heard the phrase, "don't believe everything you read." This is so true, especially in these scenarios. What I found most disturbing was the fact that the person writing this seemed to truly believe this. Yes, I have absolutely generalized the shit out of the paper written I am referring to, with very good reason—it made me angry. "If you take the drugs out of the equation, everything will be fine"—are you freaking kidding me? That's comparable to handing a revolver to someone who you know is feeling suicidal, yet not giving them any bullets and walking away. Does one truly think that if one desired—and in this case, the desire is certainly there—that they couldn't find the bullets for said revolver? Can a person that doesn't have legs for whatever reason not learn to run? I believe that's also been proven to be reality.

What we are dealing with here is the human mind, and the power of that mind. Only a very small part of the potential of the human brain has been tapped at this point, which in itself is an indescribable amount of knowledge. Yet, we can still come to the stupidest conclusions of things that have not been even remotely explored; it is incomprehensible to me. Take the drugs out of the situation and everything will be fine, my ass.

If, in fact, the addict has not yet dealt with his or her underlying issues, then I can almost guarantee with 100% accuracy that that person will either use again (and do so sooner rather than later), or spend the rest of their lives as a "dry drunk," which I will explore in Chapter 1. An angry, depressed, lonely, scared, and truly miserable person that just happens to not use anymore but truly wants to just for the sake of forgetting their deplorable existence: sounds like a wonderful life, no? Personally, I do know a few people that live their lives this way. It baffles me, yet they see no other choice. The beauty is, there *is* a choice. Do people not want to be happy? Sometimes I wonder.

I lived this way throughout my many years of addiction—only I was truly drunk most of the time, and not just wishing this to be the case. Although my previous description is extreme, it also isn't. I experienced all of these emotions and then some; I experienced them more than once, all at the same time, and even while still in the throes of my addiction.

Get this: I have had countless people say to me over the years: "Oh, you're not an addict, you just drink. People who are addicts use drugs." Oh my good God—really? This is how people perceive addiction, simply because alcohol is legal? Anyone who has ever been to a Narcotics Anonymous (NA) meeting knows full and well the "drug addict's" view of alcohol, and its extreme-alcoholism. (I have always found that words ending with an "-ism" usually lead to a scenario that one does not want to be associated with. Think about that, and draw your own conclusions; you may be surprised.)

My own addiction as such was that of alcohol. This is not to say there have not been other substances involved throughout my life; there certainly have been, but none went to the extent of my alcoholism. I was not addicted to any of the other resplendent idioms of my youth and early adult life. I was always so enamoured with the effects of alcohol that no matter what, I always returned to it. The fact that I did not realize (or want to realize—I'm still not sure which) that I was an addict prolonged my dependency. Regardless, even when becoming aware of that knowledge, I persisted. Year after year, I kidded myself that I was fine.

I continued to tell others that I did not have a problem. I lied and said I was drinking far less than I was to my bosses and friends. The amount of times that I had this conversation with an employer is staggering to me now, and oddly I managed to keep most of my jobs throughout this nonsense. Do not misunderstand me; I certainly did lose a few very good jobs, even though these employers went out of their way to try and help me in a situation when they had no obligation to do so. They valued me as an employee and wanted to help, but they also valued me as a person—that was why they wanted to help, but I could not see the forest for the trees at the time. Believe me, the shame I worked through after becoming sober relating to this was not an easy thing for me to deal with, but I did. I had let down so many people that truly cared about my well-being—people who wanted to see me get better—all for the sake of the bottle. What I have chosen to do with this book is not focus on my alcoholism per se, but on the topic of addiction itself—all addictions, as the similarities between them are, well-similar.

The addictions rehabilitation facility became my home for an extended period of time (and believe it or not, I am still closely associated with it). During my time there, I once made the very unfortunate mistake of iterating this phrase to my primary (and relatively new) counsellor: "I'm just a drinker." This was, of course, just the wrong thing to say to her, ever, at any time. It took a very long time for her to let me "live that down," and she still refers back to that moment from time to time. Thankfully, it is now an inside joke that we share. Even though it isn't very funny given the subject matter, it still makes me laugh—yet painfully so.

What is addiction? Oddly enough, the *Oxford Dictionary* has no description of the word "addiction," other than stating it is a noun (wow). Now, here's the definition for the word "addict": "noun; 1. a person addicted to a habit, drug, etc. 2. an enthusiastic devotee of a sport etc."[1]

Now, the word "addicted" is another can of worms altogether: "adjective; 1. physically and mentally dependent on a particular substance. 2. enthusiastically devoted to a particular thing or activity."[2] This is rather self-explanatory, isn't it? When it comes to personal addiction, my two biggest ones would be

---

1   *Oxford Canadian Dictionary of Current English*, s.v. "addict."
2   *Oxford Canadian Dictionary of Current English*, s.v. "addicted."

booze and work. When I said this to people, they look at me strangely and ask, "How in the hell can you be addicted to work?"

Believe it or not, it's fairly simple; I truly love what I do, and therefore I have worked myself to the point of stupidity, to the extent of complete physical and mental exhaustion. Then, to make myself feel better—to get a second wind, and quite possibly relieve the stress of an extremely stressful occupation, which I thrived in—I drank, and I drank to excess. Yet I was fine, because I was "only" a drinker; it's not an addiction, it's a lifestyle, or so I've been told. The next morning you may have a hangover depending on what you imbibed upon, yet there are no long-term, lasting effects of alcohol. Tell that to my liver; surprisingly, after thirty not-so-illustrious years of drinking, my liver is fine. But that's not the point; I was lucky. As for my heart, well, that's another story altogether. It would seem excessive drinking can cause all sorts of heart related issues, high blood pressure and coronary artery disease just to name a few that I have now been blessed with.

One of the biggest misnomers surrounding alcohol is that it is a socially acceptable pastime, and for many, a part of daily life. This is because of the general public's sheer ignorance. If you're a drunk you live on "skid row," right? So let's just ignore the problem and it will go away. Strangely, I've found that people with drug addictions are treated differently—definitely not better, yet with the acceptance of the fact that they have a problem. Even in this day and age, they are often cast out from society and treated as worthless, even though the problem is solvable. It's so nice, I know, that people just seem to not have the time to help others in need in this kind of situation; "let someone else deal with it."

Did you know that any "detox" worth being called a detox will not admit a person if their addiction is either alcohol or benzodiazepines, *unless* that person can be medically supervised during the process? It's starting to sound more like a serious issue, isn't it?

To say what it is that makes a person an addict is like playing Russian roulette for lack of a better analogy; one just never knows. The circumstances can be few, or they can be many, and what makes one person an addict may not have any effect on another whatsoever. Again, this predominantly goes back to the human mind and how each and every individual perceives the world around them, and accordingly, how they choose to deal with their own circumstances. It truly boils down to a choice, and that choice is up to each individual; we, believe it or not, choose to be addicts. As harsh as it sounds, no one is holding a gun to our heads and *forcing* us to use; we make that choice all by our lonesome, because we lose our rationality in the grip of addiction. If they fail to realize that they have a problem, most addicts will continue to use. This is the power of addiction; it is intense, regardless of the substance of choice. The only way to overcome the addiction is to once again return to the rational mind and reinvest in its power. When coherent, the mind is so very much stronger than the addiction, and when the mind is free of the substance—not completely (that's what detox is for), but rationally—a choice can be made.

Hence, while it's not easy, stopping is an attainable goal that has been accomplished by many an individual in many different fashions, and it's all based on one's thinking. The power of addiction is very strong but the power and the will of the human mind is so much stronger; all that is needed is the understanding of how to harness this resource and use it to one's benefit instead of one's self-destruction.

"Awareness" is a word I cannot state often enough. There is a great need to have self-awareness, self-discipline, and self-control in order to overcome addiction. However, before any of this can happen, we have to admit to ourselves that we have an addiction; then we can start exploring why it is that we became addicts in the first place. To some, this may not be something they ever wish to conclude. I, personally, will keep looking at my own issues, and I will keep discovering—such is my nature. I believe it is very unlikely that I or anyone else will ever come to a definite, scientific conclusion as to why addiction occurs. There are theories, ideas, and hypotheses galore. I believe it is simply too broad and expansive a subject. I may be wrong, and as such I shall personally continue my journey of self-discovery because I know it can do me no harm. Who knows, someday I may find an answer as to why I have the addictive personality I do instead of just theories, but I doubt it. And you know what? I'm just fine with that.

Chapter 1

THE DRY DRUNK

THIS BEING a book about addiction, I am sure some are wondering why I would begin with the topic of a drunk; after all, drinking is only a singular addiction, correct? It's true; a drunk is a drunk, although a "dry drunk" is something utterly different. A dry drunk can be a person that is an alcoholic, sure, but usually it is much, much more than just that. The reasoning I have for starting with the subject at hand is simply because I have a lot of experience with this. To be frank, I see this on a daily basis; this is not something I aspire to watching firsthand.

It is honestly a very painful thing to behold, especially daily, especially when there is no need for it to happen, especially when it is such an easy thing to realize, and when I truly believe it is harder to be "dry drunk" than it is to be an actual drunk. Let me explain: the only real qualification for being an alcoholic is being able to purchase a bottle—and that's a bottle of *anything*, trust me on this one. There is very little intelligence involved.

Someone who is classified as a "dry drunk" really has to work at being such. It is not an easy task to keep oneself in such a state of denial, depression, and self-loathing for an extended period of time. The thing about this affliction is that a dry drunk does not usually know they are suffering, hence the DENIAL acronym. My interpretation of "denial" is one that refuses to acknowledge or accept that one has a problem in the first place- in many cases it is both.

My interpretation of a dry drunk is a person who is a recovering addict of any description; the type of addiction doesn't matter at all, the term simply refers to an addict that is no longer using their drug of choice, yet they are not receiving the support or the counselling (or even the methadone, in the case of the recovering heroin addict). They have gone as far as removing the drug from their lives, yet have not attempted to get help in the form of counselling or support to ensure they can cope with the loss of whatever the drug of choice happened to be. If it was gambling, then there's Gamblers Anonymous, and if it was sex, Sexaholics Anonymous (and yes, there is such a group).

In the many attempts that I made at sobriety—and for me it was the booze alone—I tried to do it alone. It doesn't work. You cannot just quit and expect for everything to be fine. To begin with, people use for a reason, and although it may all be in good fun to begin with, usually we continue to use for an underlying reason or circumstance that we either are or are not aware of. Each person is going to differ in some way, shape, or form, just as each person is different from the next. As a general rule, people are very ignorant, and I say that with love. We tend to believe that if we happen to know a little bit about a subject—whatever that subject may be—then that makes us an expert on that particular phenomenon. We really do, as foolish as it sounds. We are a race of know-it-alls.

One of my theories on addiction is that we forget the knowledge we do have, the knowledge that we worked so hard to acquire throughout our lives. It truly seems so much easier for the average person to just forget about their troubles for the time being and place themselves in another realm, another reality, and another sense of self. In the short term, this really is rather harmless. If it persists, we sink deeper and deeper into the addiction, usually without any knowledge that we are doing so.

In the case of the dry drunk, we stop by using the "cold turkey" method and expect that we will just go on being ourselves. Some of us knew that we were addicts going into this; others do not. Some that *know* they are an addict have no idea how much of an addict they are. Some think that they are no longer an addict because they no longer use.

Of course, all of these assumptions are inherently wrong. The first thing one has to do is to admit to themselves that they are an addict to begin with, and until this happens, the "dry drunk" scenario is going to play a role. Step One of the Alcoholics Anonymous guidebook to celestial freedom is the following: "We admitted that we were powerless over our addiction—that our lives had become unmanageable."[3] Without this admission, you are fighting a losing battle.

My intention is not to preach the *Big Book*, as you may have noticed. It is not for everyone, yet it does work for a lot of people every day. That's the key here: "one day at a time." Personally, I no longer go to meetings. That being said, it is not because I do not believe in the concept; I do, although the meetings

---

[3] Alcoholics Anonymous, *Big Book*, 4th ed. (Alcoholics Anonymous World Services, 2001): 59. http://www.aa.org/pages/en_US/alcoholics-anonymous, 59

just do nothing for me. However, I strongly believe in the entire concept of the Twelve Steps and the twelve-step process. It does work. I do not believe I would be where I am today without the step work I have done and continue to do to this day. The dry drunk has none of these resources.

Another form of support is just that—support, such as another person to talk to. Sometimes that's all it takes, just to not lose sight of the fact that you are an addict. To believe that you have miraculously been cured is completely foolish, especially if you have never even admitted to yourself that you have a problem. My ex-wife, for example, was a person that was able to just quit and never ever have another drink. I have always had a very hard time accepting this. I would accuse her that she was never truly an alcoholic because she was able to do this. One of the reasons our marriage broke up was because of this tension. How could she never need any form of support whatsoever? This made no sense to me. Sure, I was still very heavily into my addiction at the time, but I knew enough about how the entire recovery process worked to feel that this was not right. I was not aware of the support system that she did have, simply because it did not have a name or a place. It was not meetings and *Big Book* studies and counselling; for her, it was her family. Her support system was her family, plain and simple. She absolutely was an alcoholic; she just dealt with the situation in the fashion that was the best fit for her at the time. I, however, had not yet realized the extent of what a "support system" could be.

It was during these times that I came to the realization of what a "dry drunk" was because I was living the life of one. I suffered from depression to the tenth degree, yet I was unaware of it. I was incessantly angry, yet I was unaware of that too. I had no appetite, which for me was nothing new, simply because I was an alcoholic. I hated myself, but was also blind to it. I was ridiculously underweight and I thought I looked fine. Being a very vain person this should have been a dead giveaway to me. Thinking I looked "fine" was the addiction talking, not my rational mind, nor my cognitive sense of being. I walked around constantly complaining about how horrible my life was and how much I hated my job. Guess what? I did not even know this was the way I was behaving. These are just a few of the behaviours that a dry drunk will exhibit without even knowing they are doing it. This is frightening, no?

I can honestly say that I do not blame my ex-wife whatsoever for leaving, as she did. Jesus, I am a very, very patient man, yet I do not know how much of that nonsense I could have put up with.

So to say that these are the only characteristics of the dry drunk is not the case; they are just the only ones I was aware that I was suffering from at the time. Of course, there are many more. Thinking that everything is okay is usually the biggest fallback of an addict, especially at the beginning of the process.

People by nature are just incessant about the time factor; the saying "there is no time like the present" comes to mind. Sure, that works when you finally admit that you *do* have a problem, but to say to yourself, "Okay, I am going to be finished the recovery process in let's say, three months, so hold on to your knickers, Billy," it doesn't really happen that way. If you are certain about your choice to be clean and sober for the rest of your life, well, that's how long it is going to take. Like it or not, you are in this for the long haul, otherwise it just is not going to be successful.

One must really touch on denial here also; simply not realizing what the hell is going on is really beside the point. If you have admitted to yourself that there is a problem, now the whole idea is to gather as much information on the subject as humanly possible and continue on from there. The more information you have, the more people you can consult, the better.

Truthfully, there is never enough people you can talk to while going through this. As with most things in life—be it work or play or just the day-to-day nonsense of reality—the more help you have, the better. The more information you have the better, as to just go with the smallest or least amount of knowledge will do you no good in your endeavours. I have always been one to do things well, otherwise

I get no satisfaction from the attempt. What's the point of doing something half-assed?

I remember this one time I had decided to stop drinking, sort of just on a whim. I did, yet I didn't go to any meetings simply because at the time, many years ago, I had no real understanding of the twelve-step process. I did go to this group session twice a week for two hours at a time simply because I knew I needed something more, and that I could not do this completely alone. The thing about it was that without any further support after this group, the only thing I wanted to do was drink. Why? The mind is programmed to perform certain tasks and daily events; for me, it was to drink. When I did stop, I had nothing else to fill up the timeframe that I used to spend with my friend, the bottle. Of course, this bout with sobriety did not last a terribly long time. In the evenings, I drank. The next morning, I would go to this group that was "helping" me, swear to myself that I would not leave this day and go and do the same damn thing, and like clockwork I would leave the group and make a beeline straight for the liquor store. It was almost as if I was in a trance; there are so many times that I truly do not remember either entering the liquor store or purchasing the bottle, how in the hell I got to the store in the first place, or how I got home afterwards. Quite simply, I wasn't there. I was on a sort of autopilot; my subconscious mind had overtaken my physical body and I didn't know where or what I was doing.

Anyone can go to meetings and to counselling yet still be a dry drunk. Seriously, I may not seem to be giving anybody any sense of hope here yet, but believe it or not I am. I have been through this entire process more than once so I know. The main problem is making the decision to stop and thinking *that's it, I'm done, let's just move on.* To go to the meetings and the counselling sessions alone is also not enough; this *will* be a constant for the rest of your life. Once we realize this, once a plan is in place, only then can we really move on with the self-assurance that we are on the right path. Again, this does by no means negate the fact that a relapse may happen. It can, and it does. Most people having this experience will unfortunately take this as a sign of failure and give up, but they're wrong; this is not a failure. It is simply a slip, and it does not mean we should just give up and throw away everything that we have done to this point. It's just a slip. Many people experience a slip and for many it only re-enforces the will to try harder, it does not mean the end of the world, we pick ourselves up and dust ourselves off and try again. As discouraging as this can be it can also be looked at as an awakening.

Chapter 2

THE NEXT STEP

AFTER BECOMING sober, I (like many others) thought *Hey, now that I'm sober, I'm fine, and everything will be okay because I have willed it to be so.* Sorry, but that doesn't work. This is the time to really start to put the plan I mentioned into perspective. Having a set recovery plan in place is a huge part of this process, without this the odds of failure are going to be much greater. This is not an easy task, yet it's definitely one that needs to be completed for the sake of your long-term success. At this point, you may think that being clean and sober is the biggest pain in the ass you have ever experienced in your futile existence. At this point, you would not be incorrect in this assumption; it truly is a ginormous pain in the ass, and guess what? *It gets harder.* Yes, this is where the whole process becomes more difficult before it gets any easier. You have been forewarned, and I wish you the very best of luck. Even if everything is properly executed, it will—without a shadow of a doubt—have some downsides to it.

Think of this next step (or bunch of steps, for that matter) as the beginning of a new life. I did, and I found that with this in mind it became a bit easier to handle. I knew that I no longer wanted to live my life the way I had been, and all I wanted to do was change.

Do not misunderstand me; for the most part, my life had not been a horror show—it had been good. I had accomplished many things that I am still very proud of to this day and would never want to change. However, when I started the spiral of destruction that was my addiction, the entire world went to shit—uncontrollably so. I had absolutely no idea what was happening to me simply because I was blind to it. It wasn't that I was completely oblivious, but I hadn't yet reached the stage where I was able to admit to myself that I was, in fact, an addict.

Now we have the admission behind us—moreover, right smack in front of our faces. We have admitted we were powerless; okay, now let's deal with a way out. One of my first very stupid mistakes was to isolate myself. Don't do this. Even though you may feel as if the entire world is against you at this particular juncture—and some of that world very well may be—there are people out there that can help. This is the next step, and this will not be easy either, but the need to seek out people who you can talk to is tantamount to an extended recovery.

I cannot stress this enough: you cannot go this alone. It may seem that I keep mentioning this little tidbit of information, but I do simply because of the importance here. At first you may think there is no one who understands; I sure did. Find a person who can fully understand your addiction, even if you don't have any idea of why you are an addict to begin with. That is not of much importance right now—possibly in the future, but not now.

There are many programs that are available to the everyday individual concerning addictions rehabilitation; unsurprisingly, they are not advertised as well as the latest Quentin Tarantino flick. You need to dig. Many are government-run and government-funded—although being the government, they are not about to just throw these secrets around to the common man (as they should); after all, that is why we pay taxes. That topic would be another book in itself, anyway.

My suggestion is to find a program—any program—and a place where there are others who are going through a similar situation; it helps to be surrounded by people who you can relate to, and they can also relate to you and your experiences. One thing many addicts tend to forget very easily is that they are not alone in this; so many people suffer from addiction issues, every single one for their own reasons. You truly are not alone in this, so why go there to begin with? Get out and meet people in the same scenario, no matter how painful it may seem at first; just remember they are probably now—or at some dissolute point, were—feeling the exact same way.

In this respect, what I did was enter what I believed to be a ninety-day treatment program in the greater Vancouver area. When I say "believed," that was the initial idea I had: ninety days of counselling in a live-in environment in the downtown eastside of Vancouver. Let's just say I ended up staying for a full fourteen months for a program that is ninety days; one could say I was very determined to get this right. Having said that, this is the best thing I could have possibly done for myself at the time. Because of my own sense of focus and commitment to all things recovery I was—and continue to be—very successful.

Success only happens for a small percentage of those who attempt recovery, and I cannot change that—only each individual can. This is where the determination comes into play. Many people are certainly qualified to help you with the "tools" you need to succeed, yet it will not be handed to you on a silver platter. The work is your own, the pace you set is your own, and of course, the means by which you choose to accomplish this is your own. This is the program I chose, and it was exactly what I needed.

There are many reasons why it took me so long to find treatment, and sometimes it wasn't my fault (I will not use names so as to protect the innocent and all that horseshit). The program I took was through the Salvation Army. I thought it was odd that I had never even heard that this program existed; I had been looking for something along these lines for a great number of years. It bothers me that I had gone to the government many times asking for their assistance in finding treatment, but this program was never once mentioned. I know they are very aware of its existence, as they paid for my stay for the fourteen months. I shall always wonder how it was that this program was overlooked in the past—that's my beef, though. Once a person has admitted they have a problem and are actively seeking help, my hope is you will not experience as many roadblocks as I came upon.

Now I will give you insight into my recovery story. It was May 30, 2014—the day I arrived on the doorstep of the Salvation Army. To say the least, I was terrified. I was hung-over; my clean date was the 27th, so I really had only been sober for less than three days. This is not the way they would normally accept someone. I must have fooled them from the get-go—or did I?

After I got a bed, I promptly admitted my sobriety date, which needs to be at least seven days clean and sober. I had already been admitted by this point; they realized right away how serious I was about this whole thing, and so they let me stay.

Honesty from the beginning of the recovery process is the best for everyone involved. In fact, if the people who are trying to help you cannot trust you from the start, then you may as well just go back to your drug of choice right now. It will not work without honesty—complete honesty. One cannot be just a little—or even a lot—honest; I believe the term is "full disclosure." This may be difficult initially, as it was in my situation, which may not be yours. These were professionals I was dealing with in the field of addiction. There was probably nothing I said that they have not heard at least once. I was not about to surprise anyone. Honesty is the best policy, as we all learned from our parents or grandparents.

Now, keeping in mind this is the way I proceeded (and I shall keep iterating this throughout), there are many other courses of action should live-in treatment not be a good fit. However, what I will also keep repeating is this: if you feel recovery is not for you, then you are not ready for this. Don't waste your money on this book when you could use that cash for another fix—you are not doing me or yourself any favours here. Overcoming addiction is all about sacrifice, change, and admitting that we have to make amends for our wrongs; going in with gun blazing—although it sounds good—will not last. Time, sweet precious time, is what you need. Recovery is a slow and painful process that will last for the rest of your existence. So suck it up, Buttercup.

As you may now realize, I personally used humour throughout my initial recovery. Not all people understand my sense of humour, as it tends to be rather dry at times, but it helped for me, and it was a coping mechanism. When I was upset I would make light of the situation until such a time as I could process what was upsetting me for the longer term.

This is another learned ability: processing what one learns about one's self throughout recovery. So much information is available—and is needed—for one's success. It can be likened to going to university for your master's degree in Addiction Recovery. It may even lead to gainful employment—you just never know. However, if used too frequently, humour as a coping tool can also be detrimental; it can cause you to isolate yourself and avoid the real issues at hand. There is a very fine line here. This is another prime example of why you need people to talk to, regularly and often.

Now is the point in your recovery process when you need to start building a network of people—suitable people—who you can talk to whenever you feel the need arise. Being a relatively shy person myself, I found this very difficult. I can say that I was very blessed with the initial counsellor I found in this program. Good addictions counsellors are very hard to come by, but they are alive and kicking; you just need to find one who you connect with, and you truly will be off to the races. I could say I got lucky; however, I believe it was partly fate that I found the counsellor I did—no lie. I had previously seen at least twelve others (quite possibly many more than that, as I lost count). Again, not finding what you are looking for right away does not mean you should give up. If you do, you weren't ready, anyway.

This program I took was very in-depth. The structure was as such that there was rarely a moment to have to yourself. In the beginning, this is a good thing; it is difficult to use if you do not even have the time to think about it, let alone go out and score. People still managed to do it though, more often than you would imagine. It was baffling how some people managed to do this in a residential treatment facility, but it happened. I will not say that the program was comparative to being incarcerated, but it was rather regimented starting off. We were told when to eat, when to attend sessions, seminars, and groups, and when we had free time. In the pre-treatment phase we tended to rely on the buddy system because we had to, but gradually we came to understand the value in that system in regards to staying clean and sober. The value of having that other person to talk to—even though you knew nothing about them—had its genuine comforts. The program was set up to keep us busy enough until such a time that the physical cravings began to diminish; by then we (hopefully) found other things to fill the time-void that was previously entrenched with using. This was the essential intent—to replace the time we spent destroying ourselves with time relating to our new recovery plans.

Chapter 3

DISCOVERY

Throughout the course of our lives we have all had and made various discoveries. As a child, the things we discovered were tantamount to our growing. We discovered that if we put our hand on the stove we got burned. It was simple; we just don't do that again, right? We discovered that falling out of a tree is painful—it really hurts—and our mind told us that maybe that was not such a good idea. So why is it when we become adults we do persist on doing things that are inherently harmful to our well-being? Ironically, this can be because the initial euphoria we receive from these acts of indiscretion is wonderful. We simply are not thinking long-term. This is, of course, where these acts can turn into addiction.

Do not take this the wrong way, but I have found over the years of my addiction that when trying to clean up, most people (including myself) have absolutely no idea whatsoever *why* they are addicts. Using the word "discovery"—moreover, "self-discovery"—as a metaphor for all the things that may have been a cause to the addiction is somewhat redundant. The amount of things that I have discovered about myself are numerous in such that these were quite obviously things that I was aware of yet unaware of how they affected my everyday life. As an example, I have always been a very caring and helpful person. I would give my help to anyone who needed it—always, no questions asked. What I did not take into consideration was myself. In reality, I was never worried about me—ever. To say this had a ripple effect would be a rather large understatement.

Not thinking of myself and overthinking everyone else's problems to the point where they began to affect my well-being, I got into my own sense of disillusionment. I worried about how things were affecting everybody else, and when I started to feel the world had dealt me a bad hand—even though I was dealing with the problems of others—I dealt with the stress and pressure of these situations by drinking, a lot. No wonder I became an addict . . .

In fact, when I "discovered" this about myself, I was in awe of myself. Not because I was a nice person for helping others; not at all, because I was so naïve as to the way in which it had and would affect me. It just did not occur that this could be detrimental to my own self. All I had really ever known from the time I was a young boy—what I was taught as a child as most children are, I believe—was to help your fellow man. How in the hell could this have turned me into an addict? The truth is, it didn't—I did it all by myself. I have an addictive personality, as many people do. This was another huge discovery for me when it happened. I also came to understand that I was a perfectionist, perhaps obsessive-compulsive, and that I hated change.

I hated change? I honestly had no prior knowledge of this. Hell, my life has always been in a constant state of change, since the time I was a young boy. Our family was constantly moving, constantly changing schools, rarely staying in one town or city for more than a few years, constantly having to make new friends, having to leave good friends; how in the hell could I not like change?

It is odd to me that now that I have discovered this, I embrace change, and I look for it. I cannot say I always enjoy life's shifts, but who does? It is the discovery of new things about one's self that is the key here. Many of the discoveries I have come to find about myself I will say were not very pleasant to begin with. If a person truly wants to change, then they need to discover exactly what it is that is holding them back from doing so.

Many of the things that I did discover about myself I just kind of stumbled upon—or so I thought. I was wrong; I learned all this because of the counsellors who were a part of the program I was involved with. My primary counsellor led me to discover things about myself that she knew were perhaps an issue without me ever being aware of them. It was not until we had been seeing each other in our client/counsellor relationship for some time that she made me aware of this little tidbit of self-knowledge. We had a good chuckle over my revelation.

She was also the one who led me to the realization that I was a perfectionist. Although perfectionism in itself is not necessarily a bad thing when it's mixed with the other redeeming qualities I had, it does tend to become somewhat overwhelming. One can load way too much information into one's head all at the same time, frighteningly so.

So where am I going with all this fluff? To fully understand the way we work-we have to understand ourselves from the inside out. What is it that really makes us tick, and who is our inner being? Sounds like a heap of clichés, doesn't it? A bunch of hooey, perhaps? But seriously, if you are unaware of what it truly is that makes you act the way you do, what makes you respond in a certain fashion, and what it really is that makes you *you*, how can you expect to know what it is (if anything) that needs to be changed or worked upon? Think about it for a minute. Quite obviously, no one is perfect—except me, of course, but I have been working on this a long time, no really if I was perfect I would not have found myself in this treatment program to begin with.

Seriously, everyone has things about themselves they wish were different, and this is the perfect opportunity to take that journey of self-discovery. What truly is it that we wish to change? And why do we wish to change those things in particular? We, ourselves, are the only ones who can answer those questions. This is the time to take a thorough look at yourself and come to some conclusions as to how those changes can make you a better person, to give you the opportunity to live a much more fulfilling life and lifestyle. Imagine this: the possibilities are truly mind-boggling.

When I first started my journey I literally had no idea what it was I was about to discover. For all intents and purposes, I was what I will call a "lost soul." My life had become such that absolutely nothing mattered to me except the bottle; it controlled my being. Everything I did and said in some way, shape, or form related to the final outcome at the end of my day—which was, of course, to become utterly obliterated.

I am still quite taken aback of myself every time I think of this, every time I realize just how very strong the draw of the addiction was. I was hypnotized to its total destructive hold over my sense of self. I would go through my day as any other person would; if I was working, I would go to work, do my job—and do it well, I must say—finish my workday, and go home and do whatever. The point is that throughout the course of that day, subconsciously, I would be plotting as to how I was going to be able to purchase that bottle of "release" at the end of the day. I was planning which liquor store I was going to spend those hard-earned dollars at, and what time I would go, to the point where I knew where and when I would be able to consume the very first drink of the day. The addiction was all-powerful for me, and I had absolutely no control; these were my thoughts, and always my thoughts. If I had no money, I would find a way to solve this so that I had enough to buy that bottle. To me, it did not matter whether I ate or not. Many times I would not pay my rent on time for the sake of having one more night of relief from the pain that defined my life. Depressing, isn't it? So now imagine how I felt when I was hammered across the back of the head with this self-discovery. This was very hard for me to digest at first. To say I was "gobsmacked" would be an understatement.

The idea that becoming drunk at the end of my day was truly all-consuming, and I had no awareness of this for a very, very long time. To me, this is just how people lived. It was almost as if after a long, hard day this was my reward, and this was normal. Everyone on the face of the planet went through this, every day, I thought. I was being normal. Of course, the discovery, the idea, the concept that this was an inherently unhealthy way to live one's life and that it was so "not normal" came as quite a shock.

This discovery was monumental for me. I needed to change this, and to discover why and what it was that had led me to these initial conclusions in the first damn place. I did not wish to be an addict any longer. Self-discovery can be a very painful thing, yet it does not have to be if handled with the knowledge that the long-term goal that you are striving for is attainable. The fact is that this is not rocket science; just as being an addict came easy, being a recovering addict can be just as easy if approached with the proper mindset.

Again, I will reiterate the value of never trying to do this alone. Seek out people who are going to be in your corner for the long-term, people who will help you discover the things about yourself that may have attributed to the addiction. Really, it doesn't matter why you became an addict in the first place, but knowing how to continue on without the substance is the key. The longer my sobriety lasts, the more I learn about myself. Having a clear mind and the willingness to be open to anything must be present for success.

When people speak of core beliefs and values, what they are referring to is not what life is all about, but instead what the *individual* is all about, deep down. So much of life as we know it today is unfortunately about what other people think of us as a person. If someone doesn't like me as a person I will wonder why it is they feel that way, but truthfully, it no longer nags at my soul as it once did. I discovered that my feelings and my emotions are as important—if not more so—than those of others. I discovered that I matter as a person. The truth is that not everyone has the same lack of self-confidence as I had at one time. It still comes up and bites me on the ass from time to time, yet I recognize it when it does and act accordingly.

I am not the all-seeing guru, but the discoveries I have made by just being open and honest with others and myself have led me to a much better place. I know what makes me "tick," for lack of a better phrase. What I am now doing is giving to myself, for myself. The discovery of giving to others alone with no regard to my own needs had a profound effect on the way I would continue with this journey of mine. Now, I am giving to others the knowledge I gained in my recovery because I want to, not because I feel this is what I need to or should do. I believe this may be why I was put on this planet to begin with.

One might say that I have a very grand interpretation of my self-worth, but during my addiction I was destroying just that: my self-worth.

For the most part, the way that each and every person chooses to live their lives is completely up to the individual. If someone chooses to be a lonely, bitter person, then they will be just that. It is not just due to circumstance; no one has to live a miserable existence if they do not wish to. The key is to learn how to become content in one's own skin. This involves a bit of self-discovery.

Chapter 4

DEPRESSION

Depression is a topic I am well-versed in as I have suffered personally. It is another one of those disorders that tends to sneak up on someone, even if they have no prior knowledge that this was even an issue. Unfortunately, there are things in this life that are very depressing; even though a normal person does not really know the meaning of the word, it is an all-too-common occurrence. Clinical depression, for instance, is something that is very rarely diagnosed properly because of the complexities in doing just that. Having been declared clinically depressed in the past, I certainly know the given parameters of this mysterious yet very common condition. This is definitely not something one just wakes up with. Depression is a slow and gradual condition that, over time, can turn into much more than just lethargy and listlessness.

One of the many symptoms I had were mood swings, which were at times catastrophic in their intensity. I experienced anger (normally, I am not an angry person), no energy, a lack of focus on anything, lack of appetite, and many others that are way too numerous to list. During my mood swings, I would be the happiest person one minute and then, for no apparent reason, I would become the exact opposite— so very unhappy, yet I had no idea why. Sometimes this is what would anger me, simply because I did not understand what it was that was going on in my own head. The idea of not understanding one's own feelings was catastrophic for me. It meant that I was not in control any longer, so I would turn to the only thing I knew for solace, which of course was alcohol. The lack of an appetite was what led to my lack of focus, and also my lack of energy. As we all know, without proper sustenance the body will just not perform the way it is supposed to.

Now, these little facts about my symptoms aren't mind-boggling, yet at the time I had absolutely no idea I was creating a fair amount of my suffering myself. Depression is something that is not only very hard to understand from the perspective of the one with the affliction, but the symptoms are also hard to place.

Having said that, if you feel as if you may have any of these symptoms, then by all means bring it up with your doctor. For me it really was a catch-22; I drank because I was depressed, yet alcohol is a serious depressant, so which is the lesser of the two evils? I could not find a happy medium at the time, so I opted for both. It wasn't really a very wise decision in hindsight.

Honestly, I had no idea I was depressed; my then-wife pointed this out to me as a possibility. She thought it may have been an issue and asked if I would consider talking to someone about it; at the time, it did seem like a good idea. This was at a time that I had previously decided to try and deal with my addiction issues, but mostly for the wrong reasons; those reasons were for the benefit of others, and not for myself, which (if you have not learned this already) is inherently wrong. I was trying to save what was left of our relationship, and not trying to make myself well first before attempting something as complex as a relationship.

Depression is one of those things that people seem to keep quiet about, usually because there is so little that is known about the issue. Nowadays, it is actually considered a mental disorder that can be regulated with medication. One thing I learned from this entire experience was that the medications—if given properly, because there are as many different types of medications as there are forms of depression—can and do work very well. It is a matter of the right medication and the right dosage, along with proper sleep, diet, and work schedule, as well as all of these mixed into one neat little package. Choosing a medication can be very complicated, yet if all the factors are met sufficiently, then success can almost be guaranteed.

Of course, along with this is the feeling of euphoria a person can get from the medications, which in itself can alone lead to relapse (I am sorry to say). Yes, I did go there; I became even further depressed, sinking deeper and deeper into both my addiction and my state of unsettled angst. I do not remember this as a very "pretty" place in my life.

It came across to me that the further into the depression and the alcoholism I sank, the less I considered it to be a problem; I couldn't even think straight to begin with. This was a point in my life that I would rather forget completely, and this is why I *do* talk about it. Going back to the self-discovery angle, we need to remember where we once were in order to ensure that we never go to those places again. We must be aware of what brought these feelings to light; then we can acknowledge the complexity of the issues surrounding such times. Every time we delve into the same scenarios, we can and *will* find new information on why we were there in the first place, ever-strengthening the hope for a sober life. It may sound like an ass-backwards way of going about things; in order to forget, we must remember. Believe it or not it helps, it works, and it works well.

Once I did finally realize just how seriously depressed I was, once my doctor invested enough time in me, and once I was willing to admit that I had a serious problem and I needed some very serious help, then and only then could I even begin to understand what it was that I needed to do. This same doctor gave me his time because he believed I could be successful. Between the two of us, we managed to get me on the proper dosages of anti-depressants, a healthy diet, and a regular sleep and work schedule. He also signed the documents to get me into a rather intense thirty-day treatment program—one that was highly recommended with a waiting list as long as my arm. However, I was lucky to get accepted earlier than expected through a cancellation.

I can honestly say that I was doing very well at this point. The medication seemed to be working, I was happy, and I was doing the work, even though the program was not really to my liking at first. I did miss my family, but that should not surprise anyone; at the time I had a daughter that was only six months old. What could possibly go wrong at this point? You would think I was on my way to a better life; it certainly seemed that way to my now-ex-wife and I (this is what's known in the writer's world as "foreshadowing"—just sayin').

This is where this chapter gets a tad depressing. What happened next can only be a bad thing, and yes I did relapse, and I relapsed hard. To this day, I am still not certain of what the trigger was, but you know what? It really doesn't matter one bit. It happened, and it was Depression 101 all over again. I had stopped taking the medications altogether, I was drinking again, I was out of work, and I was not able to see my child for the most part. The doctor that had invested so much time in me was now refusing to see me at all, and just in case you had not figured this part out, my wife had also left me. I was in a very bad place. Surprisingly, though, I was not suicidal, so I had that going for me.

In the situation that I now find myself—twenty months clean and sober, with fourteen of those months spent in intensive therapy—one of the things I still do and will *continue* to do is to reflect back on these ridiculously depressing times that I have experienced. My reasoning for this is that every single time that I do, I learn something new about myself regarding the way in which I handled (or in most cases, dis-handled) the situations, and I learn more and more about myself. I learn how to cope in the here and now from the mistakes I have made in the past. I know I cannot change the past, and for the most part I do not wish to, yet I can still learn a great deal from it. This benefits me in my continued recovery, and also allows me to help others.

I believe I know a lot about depression, and I have written about my experience with it. However, this does not mean that I am an authority on the subject, and that was not my intent here. I do still have the occasional bout from time to time, although now I know when the effects are present and I can deal with them as they come. Having a self-awareness of the condition before it can take its hold on your psyche makes a huge difference.

Simply because a person has been diagnosed with clinical depression usually doesn't mean they will be on medication for the rest of their lives. This is something that needs to be dealt with through a medical professional, and not by just reading a damn book or two. This is a real medical condition, despite some beliefs suggesting otherwise. Again, there is no "MD" after my name on the cover, and please keep this in mind; I am not a doctor, just a man who has lived a rather colourful and full life and experienced all of the things I am speaking of in this book in one form or another. This does not make me an authority on any of these subjects.

The realm of depression can be a very scary thing for most people, as it was for me. I felt completely lost in my everyday happenings; I felt as if no one at all cared about me, or the things that happened to me. I truly felt that I was alone. The truth was I was *not* alone at that time in my life; I had a beautiful baby girl and a wife who cared for me deeply, yet I could not seem to bring myself out of the funk I was in at the time, no matter what it was that I tried. I had a good job and I had good friends, yet I felt so very lonely and it was hard for me to believe otherwise. I was also reluctant to get a doctor to weigh in on the topic. When I finally did find the help and the people that I needed in my life, I blew it all for the sake of the addiction. One can probably see just how very depressing that could become, for not only me, but also those around me who had done so very much to try and help.

What I found the most depressing about this entire time of my life was this: when I did get out of the program—which I was doing so well in—I relapsed, and it took another twenty years to pull myself out again. This was the hardest thing that I had ever done, and I know now that this will be the hardest thing I will ever have to do in my entire life, simply because I am now of the mindset that I know I could never consciously put myself through that path of self-destruction again without very dire consequences; I would not be so lucky to succeed again. Determination is so much more enjoyable than depression any day of the week. It is harder, yet it does get easier in the long-term.

I truly do wish I had some easy fix for someone dealing with depression, yet the fact of the matter is there *isn't* one. Depression can and does manifest itself in so many forms, and for various reasons, which are going to differ greatly between people. There may be some initial similarities during the outset, but that is usually where these likenesses end. What I may find depressing, another person may find invigorating; it really can be that complex and that simple at the same time.

Additionally, each and every person will always have different perceptions of a particular incident; some of these differences might be quite small. However, what is seemingly "small" to one person may be enormous to another—this is personal perception, and this is the essence of depression. Who knew depression had an "essence"? Now as confusing as those last couple of lines may seem, it really isn't if you break it down into simple semantics.

Once realizing the simple fact that depression is what you are dealing with, each and every individual can then proceed with this self-awareness and concentrate on pinpointing what it is that is the cause of the depression in the first place. Easier said than done, I know, yet this is the "essence" that I am referring to. For instance, my main source of depression was the alcoholism. It was that simple; if I stopped drinking, the majority of my depression would have abated.

Stopping the drink was not really the difficult part; for me, the harder part of quitting was the understanding of *why* it was I drank in the first place. Initially, I could not understand, which exasperated my depression further. I am of a rare breed in this respect, I believe—I'm someone who needs to know the meaning of the world around me in all of its intricacies, yadda yadda. Having the ultimate knowledge of existence is really not on most people's minds. Hence, once we understand what it is that is depressing us, we can deal with these circumstances accordingly. Finding the right person to talk to—perhaps a counsellor or a doctor who specializes in the issue of depression—is tantamount.

Many times it can be as simple as a lifestyle change, but for me, it was my entire being. Do not misunderstand; I am still the same person I was when I started this entire recovery scenario. What I have done is changed my focus on life completely, and I have removed the things that led me to the almighty addiction, whether it was the job, the friends, or the fashion in which I dealt with a stressful situation. Every part of my life had to be re-examined if I wanted to truly do this properly, and I was deathly aware of this going in. However, it does not have to be this difficult. For most it won't be, but the key is to be open to the possibilities. Take your time.

Chapter 5

PERCEPTION

THIS IS a topic that still baffles me to this day. The differences of opinion that people have on the same subject are mind-boggling to me, and in essence, that is all that perception is. Let's think of the word "religion," for instance; how many different perceptions do you think I would get for that one word? There would more than likely be at least as many interpretations of the word as there are religions in this world.

The Oxford Dictionary also seems to have many definitions of the word "perception"; accordingly, with the theme I seem to be following:

> 1. the ability to see, hear, or become aware of something through the senses. 2. the process of becoming aware in such a way. 3. a way of regarding or understanding something. 4. intuitive understanding and insight.[4]

I must admit—upon first perusing these definitions, I was even more disillusioned than before, yet it does lead to the conclusion as to why perception can be so detrimental in any given situation. The need to fully understand the perceptions of others is such an important part of the communication process. Everyone at one time or another has had a misunderstanding. The ability to ensure that one has understood the meaning that is being conveyed— especially when addiction issues are at play—is so incredibly important.

In the instance of recovery, perception of the entire process is so different in its inception. For example, people entered the program I was in with the general idea that it is ninety days of live-in group therapy for addictions. Sounds simple enough, right?

---

4 *Oxford Canadian Dictionary of Current English*, s.v. "perception."

However, people seriously would come through the doors and think that a "live-in" program means just that; there were people who honestly thought after they checked in and got their schedules and room assignments etc. they were free to do whatever they pleased from that point on, within the parameters of that daily schedule. This quite obviously was not the case. Remember: this was a rehabilitation program. If you went there for a vacation from your addiction, you were in the very wrong place; yet people still assumed otherwise. Think about that for a minute: you have admitted that your life had become unmanageable, and then you enter treatment. Would you not think you would be at the "mercy" of the professionals at this point? I certainly did.

I will say my perceptions of the world are inherently much different than most. I have always been the type of person that ensures clarification if I have even the slightest hint I have misunderstood. For me, this goes along with my character trait of being a perfectionist. The point here is that this is where *perception* comes into play. If, in fact, you have not taken the time to ensure you understand what it is that is trying to be conveyed to you, then the possibilities of a misconception—a completely different perception—becomes all too real. It really is that simple, and the amount of times it happens is astonishing. If someone were to say to you a simple phrase such as, "I think this task is something that is way over your head," how would you perceive this? Would you think it is something that is literally "over your head?" Or, would you understand that maybe the task being asked of you is something that you will not understand because of its complexity, which of course is the intended meaning here?

This can happen in any given situation at any time, and it does. In respect to the rehabilitation program itself, one does have to understand that when people enter the program they are usually not of a stable mind, to say the least. If they have gone through the detox program, perhaps they are a little bit more on the ball—or screwed up even more than before, simply because they are now dealing with life as a sober individual, which is usually new to them. I know that when I first arrived I thought I was okay; I had been drinking three days prior to my arrival, and I assumed that yes, I was still a bit hung-over, and that it would pass in a few days. I was wrong; this, my friends, was to become the longest hangover I have ever had in my life. I hope for the sake of all that is holy that it is the last hangover I will ever experience. I swear, this "hangover" lasted for the first thirty days of my stay. Following that time period, I remember starting to feel "normal" again, but it took me some time to understand this, simply because it had been so long since I had been sober for any significant length of time. I had forgotten what normal felt like. I could not remember what life was like when I did not have a mickey of vodka (at the very least) in my system—frightening, I know.

For me to say that I fully understood what was going on in my everyday situation for these thirty days would be a lie; I did not. Truthfully, I really do not even remember most of it, as I was in a fog of sorts. Even though I was participating in therapy sessions, counselling, meetings and the like, I really remember very little. Having the structure around me was perhaps the only thing that got me through this portion of my recovery; obviously there were many times that I considered walking out the door; my perception of things gave me feelings of "this is not where I should be," which made things very difficult. Only when I was given clarification of the intended meanings of the things I had to do did I feel at ease and realize that this was the only place I needed to be.

My perception that I was "in prison" was very real and scary to me. Upon understanding that this was not the case—that I was in fact in a safe place, the safest place I could have been at the time—this eventually put my troubled mind at ease. This is where I had put myself; no one else did this to me, and I could have left at any time, unlike many others who I was in this program with. Yet this wasn't the perception I had at the time because of the addiction and the subsequent withdrawal. My thinking was so skewed that I led myself to believe that I truly was being held against my will. I *believed* this. When I arrived, I agreed to abide by the rules and regulations of the facility, yet I still had the opportunity to leave if I so chose. I somehow had become unaware of this in my state of detoxification.

Understanding others was another huge roadblock during this time, simply because of the lack of mental, emotional presence in most people I encountered. Every person in the program was going through one form of withdrawal or another. What I am going to present to you in the next few pages-a short piece I wrote while I was still in recovery. It's about an observation I made of someone else (with some observations of myself thrown in for good measure). What this will attempt to do is explain *perception*, as this is my initial perception of the person I was writing about, concluding with the actual meanings of what I observed. I had drawn these initial conclusions because of my own state of mind at the time.

> There is a woman who lives in the Downtown Eastside that I see quite regularly, and have seen throughout my time here. I am at a loss to fully explain her and her situation, simply because I do not know enough about the whole area of affliction or disease or whatever it may be called. In my understanding, the woman is delusional in the manner that she sees things

that others do not. Remembering that this is only my opinions and my observations and nobody else's, sometimes when I see her she appears completely normal, (depending on your perception of normal), and at other times I just do not know what the hell to think. I have seen her calm yet quite obviously having a conversation with one or many other individuals who are not really there. Some of these conversations get very heated. There has been many a time that I have watched her walking briskly down East Hastings literally screaming at the top of her lungs at apparently no one—or at least, that's "no one" to an observer, yet in her mind there are many people around her, and she is quite upset with them, to say the very least. It can be truly painful to watch. She is in such a state of agitation it is almost as if I can see a heart attack building up inside of her, just waiting to explode should she take the situation any further.

I think what I truly had a hard time understanding is this: to me, it is apparent she is on some form of medication; I have no idea what, but I would suspect antipsychotics, and possibly antidepressants, along with others, I am certain. The reason I think this is because I can just see her in the realm of going off the deep end so quickly from the intensity of her agitation at times. Oddly, I saw her for the first time this morning at 4:30 a.m. Every other time has been during the day, and I have never seen her after the sun has gone down. I did not realize this until I saw her in the darkness of the morning. I was blown away by how extremely calm and collected she seemed, when just yesterday afternoon she was at a point where I truly thought she was about to lose her mind. I will say that she was still moving at ninety miles an hour, but this morning she wasn't screaming.

I think my biggest questions would be the following: why is she out wandering at 4:30 in the morning? Does she not sleep (like every other person) at this ungodly hour? I suppose that this could have something to do with the medications I suspect she is taking, but only if I am correct on these assumptions. The other question would be-why is she so calm this morning? Why is she still moving at such a high speed? Where could she possibly need to be at this time of the day?

That is by no means the entire story, but rather just a snippet of such. My reasoning for including it is because it demonstrates how perception changes over time; my *current* perception of the woman and her plight are completely different from what I first believed. Some of my assumptions were indeed correct, yet they were assumptions that led me to the perception of what I believed was happening in this person's world. How could I possibly know? I do not know this woman; it was only my perception, what I saw, and the conclusions I drew with absolutely no knowledge of her situation. When this happens—not only in recovery, but also in everyday life—things usually go awry; this is the fallout from making assumptions before the truth is revealed.

My perception of this woman was that she had a mental disorder; I thought this initially, for some strange reason—a reason that did not occur to me then. That reason was because of my state of mind at the time. I wanted to find something to care about other than another person with an addiction. At that time, I really did not want to think about addiction, recovery, and the whole bloody nine yards that go along with it. It can be very taxing on a person's mind when they live and breathe this for so very long. I wanted a release, and for me it was this woman with a problem different from my own. I now know that she is an addict herself, and this was why she walked down the street screaming at no one (except for the individuals in her own little world, who only showed up when she got high). I needed for it to be something else, hence the perception I created in my own mind. Can you see how another's perception of a situation can be misconstrued to something that is completely different from reality?

This is something of a dilemma for me in my life: I care. I sometimes think I care too much. Even though there is nothing wrong with this, as a character trait this can have some consequences that can be harmful. When I had this properly explained to me I admit that I was quite dumbfounded; how could caring possibly be harmful? *Really?* The thing is, caring can be harmful when someone puts the concerns of others before his or her own. Surprisingly, this made complete sense to me. It was carefully explained to me by a source that knew exactly what she was talking about.

When I saw this woman, I had simply had enough of the recovery process. To compensate, I found something that was really of absolutely no concern to me, and I focused on it. I made up a story that was inherently wrong. I perceived an imaginary scenario because I no longer wished to deal with my own. My perception of this woman's disastrous existence gave me an out. Most times this happens because others simply do not have all the pertinent information, yet in the recovery process it is a coping mechanism for some. Again, this reality made me sit down and re-evaluate my entire sense of self. Why had I decided that I no longer wanted to give two shits about my recovery, and now my attention was once again on everyone else's problems—the exact thing that was a huge factor in getting myself addicted in the first place (as in, losing my perception of myself). I was fine; everyone else needed help, but I was fine.

It may come as a shock, but most people are generally caring individuals, they do care about the plight of others. I just happened to care too much about everyone else on the face of the earth and completely forgot about myself. When I did get to a state where life was difficult, instead of utilizing some much-needed self-care (which, of course, I knew nothing about), I drank. This was my way out. My perception was that I just needed a release, and this was the best way to go about that. I was fine.

It really is a very difficult thing to look deep into one's own psyche and discover what it is that is upsetting you. Hell, it's hard to even admit there is an issue to begin with. In resistance, our minds will perceive the easiest possible way to deal with hardships. Instead of taking a good, hard look at ourselves, we create an easy out. It only works for so long, especially if you are graced with an addictive personality.

For all intents and purposes, I do not have a mental disorder, and neither did the woman who I implanted into my life because I no longer wished to deal with my own issues. Looking back, I wonder why an intelligent human being could be so completely consumed by the substance of alcohol or any other "drug of choice" for so very long; but that is a question I may never have the answer to. At the very least, now I am in a state of mind where I can continue searching for answers if I wish, but I believe I will just "let sleeping dogs lie." The reality that has become my life is that of my own well-being; it must take precedence, and my perception of such is now to the point that I can never forget my perceptions of the past. They took me to some truly horrific places. Now, with a clear mind and conscience, I can face the world once again without having to perceive anything but reality. There is no need to make things up because of the fear of my demons.

Chapter 6

INTO THE GREAT BEYOND

I AM GOING to guess that if you are still reading this mishmash of my screwed-up life, you have a very good reason to be doing so. Having said that, and having read this, you may have come to the realization that I do not have all the answers; I certainly hope that is not what you were expecting, as I believe I made this point very clear from the beginning. Moreover, this should be a model, perhaps, of another person's intrepid course of actions and directions for you to peruse and quite possibly interject into your own plan of discovery.

Many times throughout my recovery, I have come to a place of dismay, where I believed I truly could not continue on this path any longer; I had had enough, and I just wanted to return to the life I had, the place where I felt was my home. Everything I knew was not here in this lonely location I now found myself. I could not see the forest for the trees, for lack of a better phrase, and I wanted out. But you know what? Deep down, I was so very blatantly aware of the destination this would take me to. This was an even lonelier place than where I was currently residing. Sure I could go "home" (notice that home is in quotation marks), but did I *really* have a home to go back to? Did I ever really even have a home to begin with? The more I thought about this the lonelier I became, and I was falling into a place where I honestly felt I could not proceed any longer. Not to the suicidal side of things, although for some at this point, suicide is a very real feeling and possibility.

I need to add here that I am by no means an authority on the subject of suicide. This is something that is best left to the professionals. I will say that I have had the unfortunate experience of knowing people in such a position, so I am not completely oblivious to this form of headspace. My experience with this was unpleasant, and the outcome was very difficult to deal with, yet I was still very seriously in the throes of my addiction. I would never want to have to deal with that form of depression as a sober individual. My hope is that I will never have to.

For me, the feeling of loneliness was the most significant. I was in a place where I did not think I belonged, where nothing seemed to be getting any easier, where there was no proverbial light at the end of the tunnel; hell, there wasn't even a goddamn tunnel that I could see, I was so lost. Depression was a huge factor for me, and it hurt. Not only was I of the mindset that I really had no home to ever return to, I was alone, completely and utterly alone, and it was some of the worst pain I have ever experienced in my entire life. Emotional pain is something that has a life of its own, and it's a truly a daunting place. Could I ever be happy again? It sure didn't seem so. How was I to bring myself out of this? Everything I had known in my life was gone: I had lost my home and my possessions were gone, and even though I realized they were just things, it still sucked. I had lost my job to the bottle, I had thrown away the career I had worked so hard to accomplish, my wife had left me, and my daughter wanted to have nothing to do with me. I was broken and living in a place where I knew nobody, and really didn't care to know the people I was now living with. The city I was now in was a city I had left twenty years earlier because I hated it. Truly, what in the name of all that is holy was I supposed to do?

Sounds rough eh? I shit you not, it was, for what seemed like an eternity, but it did get better. Guess how? I *made* it better. Looking back on it now, this was the hardest thing I have ever done. Was it worth it? For the most part, yes, and I say that because I often feel the need to ask myself questions such as: "What if this entire menagerie of my life had never happened?" "What if I had just become the person I should have been and never experienced the addiction in the first place?" "Where would I be now if none of this had ever occurred?"

One of my counsellors through this entire mess used to say to me, "What is the point of the what-ifs and the should-haves? Will being depressed about what the hell could have happened really make things any better than they are? *No*. So stop it!"

She really did say that to me, "*stop it!*" Seriously. I didn't appreciate this at the time, but looking back, this was very funny. To pull myself out of this was not an easy task. I needed to fully explore where it was I wanted to be, and I do not mean geographically; I mean in my head. My mind had been in such a state of denial in the first place that I knew where I needed to start, and I had done that simply by coming into the treatment program: it was the admission that my life had become unmanageable. I was now sober for some six months, so why was I so depressed? I was still in a place I didn't care to be, and the possibility of returning to my past life was just not an option any longer. I didn't even want that option; at the beginning I thought that was the goal, to get sober and go home. Guess what? I did not have a home any longer; this was my new home, only I could not admit that to myself. I still hated it here. I still do, although hate is a very strong word now. I dislike living here, not hate. Things change.

In four days, I will have been sober for twenty months. In all reality, that is not a terribly long time in the grand scheme of things, but it is an accomplishment of astounding proportions for the average individual. It is not an easy task to become a real person again when in essence all one has ever known—all *I* have ever known—was that of being a drunk. Do not misunderstand me; I have not been drunk since the day I was born, thank Christ, yet somehow it seems that way at times. I have lived my adult life as an alcoholic. I somehow managed to still make a decent living for myself at the beginning. I would realize that "Hey, maybe I need to slow down for a bit," and I did. But being of a personality that addiction was present and there was not a damn thing I could do about it except quit, it persisted. I needed to completely stop, and I just could not bring myself to come to this end denominator. That just wasn't me; all I had ever known throughout my career was that in order to have the courage and strength to carry on as I was I needed the booze. It controlled me—not the other way around.

Does one ever realize these things before they become a problem? No, that's why they call it an addiction, a problem to begin with. Guess what? Being sober for what sometimes already feels like an eternity is pretty cool. I like myself again. Still, however, there are days that I want to just get obliterated. The urges, the cravings are never going to fully disappear, and the sooner we realize this the better. There are going to be things that happen in your life that are going to make those cravings happen, and at the time you may not even realize what those triggers are. It could be something as simple as a smell, for me for the longest time it was just the smell of alcohol in any form that was a serious trigger; thankfully I realized this early and didn't let that urge lead me to places I no longer wished to be. Sometimes it's not that easy; the key is to figure out what these triggers are, and to be ready for them to occur, because more often than not they *will* occur, and they are usually going to happen at the most Godforsaken time.

Really, this is something that gets easier, yet it never fully goes away. There will always be the urges and the thoughts that seem harmless enough, until such a time as you *act* on those feelings and urges. The amount this happens is mind-boggling, frightening, and most of all a huge obstacle if you let it become that. Being aware that the urges will come is a good start, and to deal with them when they do. It does not make them any easier, just more manageable. I am now in a place where I am able to deal with all of the horseshit of the daily grind and just move the hell on. It isn't easy some days, and others it just happens without ever even thinking of taking a drink. In fact, most days the thought doesn't even enter my noggin. How, you ask? Persistence? Stamina? Unequivocal knowledge of the universe? The undisputed fact that I am smarter than the rest of the human race? Fate? Nope, none of the preceding answers have anything at all to do with it. . Some days I wonder how it is I stay sober, and then I write it off as this: the amount of work I have put into my recovery in the first place. The fact of the matter is that most people do fail the first time; I did. It isn't easy, but it is doable.

Believe it or not, I *am* happy again. There was a long span of time where I never thought I could enjoy my life if I could never again have the pleasure of leaving my senses behind and just forget about the world for a while. I have many releases that have nothing to do with drugs or alcohol or any other addiction. I'm fifty years old, and I love to colour. Who knew? Not I. I do have an artistic background, so it stood to reason that it would be something I enjoyed, but sober? That was the kicker. *I can do things that I enjoy when I am sober?* Wow. This sounds so simple on paper, doesn't it?

What it comes down to is a total restructuring of one's life. Much work is needed, but remember that the basics are already there. Many people tend to forget this little fact; we have already lived a portion of our lives—in my case, half of my life. One of my greatest fears was that I had to start my life over again. I was not up for that nonsense at all. The thing of it is you do not have to restart; you can take what you already have and incorporate that into the clean and sober realm. There are going to be things you may no longer be able to do, sure, but if so, that was probably something you didn't need anyway. If it was in fact something that was so very important in your life, then you will find a way to incorporate it into your sober life. See? Simple.

I finally did leave the treatment program after fourteen months, which was a substantially long time by most standards. As I have mentioned, most people are only there for the three months and then *whammo*, "I'm cured! Someone start the party!" All too often, this is the addictive brain taking over. People figure if they can be clean and sober for the three months, *then why can I not stay that way for the rest of my life? Better still, why can I not go out with the boys on a Friday night and just have a couple of drinks, snort a few lines, pop a couple of goofballs?* Why the hell not? Because you *can't*! Do not be a moron, you have an addictive personality, you are an addict, and you *cannot* go and have a few belts. It will not work, and this is the reality of being an addict. Sorry to burst the proverbial bubble, but it ain't gonna happen . . .

I do offer you my sincerest apologies if this is not what you expected to hear. This is the reality you are going to have to deal with on a daily basis. So why not just make the best of it? This is as good a place as any to start. Make a plan and stick to it. That may sound like a catastrophically difficult thing at this juncture, but the alternatives are not so appealing any longer, are they?

Anyway, back to me (in case you have not noticed, I tend to talk about myself a fair amount). For me I actually got to the point where I truly believed that I was boring the shit out of people. I talked constantly of recovery, and it seemed like nothing else ever crossed my lips. Absolutely every single syllable that I uttered out of my pie-hole was related to this damn recovery nonsense. How in the hell could I ever again relate to the real world? I had no clue.

It was at this time that a true friend let me in on a small secret. She said to me that whether I thought so or not, I really was an interesting person, and I did have some very nice qualities. People did like me for the person I was, and no one was telling me I bored the shit out of them because of what I believed I was doing. Think about it: I was in a recovery program for fourteen months, so one would think I would talk about recovery some, no?

I am not saying that one needs to monitor their every word of conversation for the rest of their lives; that would be idiotic. Just be aware, and nothing else.

I found that thinking of what others thought of me instead of what I thought of myself was the key. In essence, that is what got me to the point in my addiction where I completely lost control because I was too busy pleasing others. When I left the program I finally started to understand where the direction I wanted to go was. No longer did I have to think about recovery 24/7. When you live within that sort of atmosphere, you really are left with little choice. I realized there is an entire, huge world still out there for the taking. I was ready. Or was I?

Scared you, didn't I? Yes, I was ready, but this was only my approach to the whole scenario; this is not the way everybody can approach the matter of addiction. Some people only have so much time. Others, well . . . they are just not ready to put their entire being into the creation of becoming a new soul. Never before had this idea even crossed my mind, and as I have stated, I am not a completely new human being that has been recreated. I'm simply the same man with many tweaks to his infrastructure. I like to think I am turning into the man I have always wanted to be. That, my friends, has nothing to do with a monetary sense, not in the least. This is a journey of reinventing my inner being.

Quite honestly, I have no idea where the hell I am going to end up. For me, at this point in time, it is strictly about the journey itself. Every single day I find something new about myself that I perhaps could work on. I have never done this before, and I have never needed to do this before—or so I thought. Apparently, I was wrong. Now I am very much in control of my life, of my emotions, and I have a strong sense of self. If tomorrow someone throws me a curveball I know I am adept enough, I am of a mindset that I can figure things out without so much as the hint of a thought of a drink. I really like the way this is turning out, although I clearly realize this is a never-ending journey—one that I shall succeed in.

Chapter 7

THE TWELVE STEPS (AND THEN SOME)

So quite obviously, the chapter title leaves me little choice but to reiterate those immortal words from so very long ago:

1. We admitted that we were powerless over [our addiction]—that our lives had become unmanageable.

2. Came to believe that a Power greater than ourselves could restore us to sanity.

3. Made a decision to turn our will and our lives over to the care of God *as we understood Him.*

4. Made a searching and fearless moral inventory of ourselves.

5. Admitted to God, to ourselves, and to another human being the exact nature of our wrongs.

6. Were entirely ready to have God remove all these defects of character.

7. Humbly asked him to remove our shortcomings.

8. Made a list of all persons we had harmed, and became willing to make amends to them all.

9. Made direct amends to such people wherever possible, except when to do so would injure them or others.

10. Continued to take personal inventory and when we were wrong promptly admitted it.

11. Sought through prayer and meditation to improve our conscious contact with God *as we understood Him,* praying only for knowledge of His will for us and the power to carry that out.

12. Having had a spiritual awakening as a result of these steps, we tried to carry this message to [addicts], and to practice these principles in all our affairs.[5]

Over the course of many years, many people have come to the realization that these steps are not for them. The entire premise of living your life to this particular set of guidelines is just plain idiotic. There are so many ideologies in these steps that are ridiculous to the everyday individual; they are daunting to some, stupid to others, and to most rather unbelievable in their complexities. Think about it: if you are not a religious person, right away the mention of the moniker "God" is going to frighten people away. They wonder, *Who is this God person you are referring to, and why should I allow Him into my life over that of the substance that has made me feel so impervious to this overwhelming world of mine?*

The realization that this is not what is meant by the word "God" is the first step here, as this truly has nothing to do with religion, unless of course you choose it to be. It is just a guideline, and one must remember when this was written, and by whom. I will not go into all of the gory details; should you want that you could simply pick up the *Big Book* and

---

5 Alcoholics Anonymous, *Big Book*, 4th ed. (Alcoholics Anonymous World Services, 2001): 59-60.

read it again, because if you are reading this book then I am certain you already have a copy; if not, it's about time you found one. They are free, if you know who to ask. It will explain everything you need to know about Alcoholics Anonymous, its founders, its premise, and its *blah, blah blah.*

Originally the idea of the Twelve Steps was religion-based; there's no lie there. This was before the birth of the entire AA system. Bill W., one of the cofounders of Alcoholics Anonymous, was not a religious man, but in his own words,

> I was not an atheist. Few people really are, for that means blind faith in the strange proposition that this universe originated in a cipher and aimlessly rushes nowhere. My intellectual heroes, the chemists, the astronomers, even the evolutionists, suggested vast laws and forces at work. Despite contrary indications, I had little doubt that a mighty purpose and rhythm underlay all. How could there be so much of precise and immutable law, and no intelligence? I simply had to believe in a Spirit of the Universe, who knew neither time nor limitation. But that was as far as I had gone.[6]

---

6   Bill W., "Bill's Story," in the *Big Book*, 4th ed. (Alcoholics Anonymous World Services, 2001), 10.

These are interesting words, no? I almost wish I had penned them myself.

My point is that if religion is not your thing, it doesn't matter. It comes down to the belief in the higher power alone, in my eyes. In my own experiences of the entire AA perspective, I was certainly not much for the idea of religion. I was absolutely not prepared for the entire church idea and all of the surrounding philosophies of religion and the like. Like Bill, I am not a terribly religious person—actually, I am not at all religious. Do not get me wrong; I do believe there is a greater being of some description who is at work somewhere, someplace, somehow, but to boil it all down and explain this, and why the entire universe is what it is would absolutely take a fair amount of time and typing for me.

Seriously, it doesn't matter. I have a higher power; this works well for me, and it has nothing to do with religion, so if becoming a Christian or a Muslim or a Member of the World Organization of the Spaghetti-Wearing Ding-Dongs of Alberta is not your cup of tea, fear not. It's okay.

The steps themselves are what had thrown me off of the entire AA premise in the first place. I had gone to the meetings over and over. I had read the *Big Book* several times, I had asked about sponsors, I knew many people who were part of the "program," but I still did not get it. Many times I continued to go to the meetings, but afterwards all I wanted to do was drink. For me, the meetings were just so dreary and depressing, how in the hell could this help me? I wanted a better way of life, and this, to me, was not the answer. What was I missing here? So I would stop going to meetings and think *this isn't working, again*. I even tried other types and forms of meetings, all to no avail. I also went to Life Ring meetings, and they were okay; same kind of premise, different perspective, but not for me, and the meetings seemed to be few and far between. I drank. For years, I had heard of people working the steps, and I wondered *what in the name of all that is holy am I missing here?* I still didn't get it.

I need to point out again that I am a recovering alcoholic. This is, of course, the reasoning behind the references to AA, but remember: this is about the steps, *not* the particular addiction. This works for everyone, not just alcoholics (I am not sure why I felt the need to point that out yet again).

Anyway, when I finally came to understand the meaning behind "working the steps," I felt like an idiot at first for not seeing this myself, but who knows—maybe I just didn't wish to. The steps and the questions and the process for doing them had been right there in front of me the entire time. Who knew? And off I went, step by step, answering every single question one by one—more than once, in some cases—not truly understanding if I was doing this properly, or just spinning my wheels, as it were.

Of course, having the amazing counsellor that I had at the time, any questions that I had about the questions I was answering were very quickly answered by her, which really did make all the difference to me. The reality of the step work is, for the most part, an effort of revealing yourself *to* yourself, which is unlike anything you have ever done before. It can honestly scare the living shit out of an individual, depending on your circumstances, but it's well worth it in the long run, judging from my experience.

The things I learned about myself and the life I had led were at times very hard to deal with, yet truly indescribable in their solemn dissolution of one's former self—frightening at times, without a doubt. However, part of the process occurs at the end of each of the steps, and this involves the reiteration of going through your writings on them with a sponsor. This I did in a roundabout sort of way, because I did not have a sponsor at the time.

As I mentioned earlier, I was not a fan of the meetings themselves, and although I went to them, I had other ideas about the entire sponsor thing. This was more of a personal issue for me. I did not like the idea of my sponsor having to be a man. I was just not comfortable with this idea, so I did not even look. Typically, if you are male you have a male sponsor; if you are female, a female sponsor. This is not the law of the Twelve Steps; there is no such nonsense, it is just felt that because of the things that are being revealed the comfort level is better suited to someone of the same gender, that's all. I disagreed; me telling my stuff to another man just did not seem appealing to me; I felt much more comfortable revealing my inner most secrets with a woman. I certainly do understand and appreciate where the reasoning of the same-sex thing comes from, and respect that it does ring true for most.

This is where I believe the entire thing seems daunting: the first step alone is sixty-nine questions. This could turn many people against the idea completely, but it is well worth it. Remember what the first step is: "We admitted that we were powerless over [our addiction]—that our lives had become unmanageable." You've come this far now; would you really expect things to get any easier right away? You haven't really done shit yet . . . Sure, you've stopped using and are sober for the most part, so *now* is the time to shape the rest of your life in the same way, admitting your mistakes and dealing with the issues of the past for the sole purpose of being able to move on with a clean conscience. That was told to me once, and it kinda fits, doesn't it?

The second step, of course, is: "[We] came to admit that a power greater than ourselves could restore us to sanity." This is where I had more difficulty, simply because this is where the entire "God fix" comes into play. A non-religious person—an unbeliever, if you will—is most likely going to be put off by this step very quickly if it is not properly explained. Honestly, I had no idea what the hell to think when it came to a higher power; to me, this meant that I had to believe in God, and quite frankly, I simply do not. Could I do this for the sake of my recovery? I did not believe that I could; the recovery part was enough by itself at this point. When it was explained to me that it's not necessarily God who is being referred to as the higher power (unless, of course, that is what you wish), it put my mind somewhat at ease. I will say that it took me a fair amount of time to figure out what it was that my "higher power" indeed manifested itself as.

To be honest, the only way that I know how to explain this is to say that my higher power is, well, me, and as strange as it may sound, it really works for me. I have known people whose higher power was a pet rock. I shit you not. That's the thing; it really doesn't matter if it helps the situation. This requires a great deal of thought for most people, yet for some none at all.

The third step in itself is another one that scares people off, simply because the word "God" is in the step itself: "[We] made a decision to turn our will and our lives over to the care of God *as we understood Him*." "As we understood him": this means that our higher power could be a lamp, for all intents and purposes, *really*. If, in fact, you are a religious person, all the power to you, go with it.

Next, step four: "[We] made a searching and fearless moral inventory of ourselves." What the hell is that about? I wasn't too sure about this step, but I know that to have overlooked it (well, if I had even finished the program to begin with) would have made the outcome of my recovery ridiculously different than it is now. This step is truly important; it is difficult to dig deep enough for it to really have the desired effect, but this is what the entire recovery process is about: fearless searching and self-discovery on a grand scale.

Step five is somewhat of a fright: "[We] admitted to God, to ourselves, and to another human being the exact nature of our wrongs." Wow, I know, especially the other human being thing. Most people are going to ask *who?* Easy—that's the whole point, as I have said, of having a sponsor in the first place. This is where they really can come in handy, when one needs to not be judged for, shall we say, his or her past indiscretions. It can be very brutal if someone is sitting with you, thinking the entire time, *what in the name of God is freakin' wrong with this idiot?* That will not help the intensity of this endeavour very much, guaranteed.

For me, having a sponsor was one of the most freeing experiences I have ever had. I honestly do not know what else I can say about the matter. It was uplifting and glorifying, seriously. I do admit I was terrified going into it, simply because of the things

I was going to reveal to another person who had no idea whatsoever of this side of my character. That is what scared me the most; I simply did not want her to know of my demons. Even though there was really nothing mind-boggling or horrific, there were things that I was truly ashamed of, without a doubt. For me to have to admit this to another person, and to have to share my innermost atrocities to someone I had begun to care about—I was worried. I was not sure of what the outcome of this would be, and this was a difficult thing to confront. I knew without a doubt that this had to be done fully and completely if I ever wanted to properly come to terms with my misdeeds. The thing is this was only the beginning; just wait till we actually get to step nine. That's when it really gets ugly.

I'm kidding. As it turns out, my fears were unfounded. My counsellor, of course, being the consummate professional she is, took me through this (seemingly to me) painful exercise virtually unscathed. She had taken up the role of my temporary sponsor, and I am very grateful for that move on her part; I know this could have been much harder with someone I was unfamiliar with. My advice is to find someone you know well enough to be able to trust with your personal shit. Again, the reasoning behind using a sponsor really goes along with the entire "being a sponsor" thing in the first place.

The next few steps I found got somewhat easier—still difficult in their depth, yet easier.

Step six: "[We] were entirely ready to have God remove all these defects of character." This, for me, was very easy, but I can see where this could become not only confusing, but also redundant. Anybody that has completed a set of steps will notice the steps themselves seem to be asking the same questions over and over again (no, you are not the only person that has noticed this), anyone that has not completed a set, well you will notice this when you do, and this is just to put the queries into different contexts. This may become annoying, I know. I believe the reasoning behind this is—and remember, this is still my opinion—that the different contexts of the same questions are meant to elicit other responses by simply asking them again, but from different points of view. You may surprise yourself with the things that come up that you simply missed the first time, just because of the way the question was asked. There are other questions that may seem just plain stupid, but this is a process; skipping things does not help the process here. You may have noticed that I have said nothing about the God reference in this step, simply because I think I have made my point on this: do with the reference what you will. These steps are for your benefit—not anyone else's.

Step seven: "[We] humbly asked Him to remove our shortcomings." Again, I found this step to be more about self-reflection than anything. I did find it quite helpful; there are twenty-one thought-provoking questions such as, "How has my surrender deepened?" or, "Has my sense of perspective been out of proportion lately?" "Have I begun thinking of myself as more significant or more powerful than I really am?" I took it a step further in my first set of steps and decided, for some inane reason, that I was going to try and explain the seven deadly sins! Truthfully I am not completely sure of the circumstances of why I took this extra step, my counsellor had suggested reading these and I got carried away. Like I said, they are thought-provoking.

Now, step eight gets a wee bit more intense again, but if you put this into the proper perspective, in many respects you should have already done a large part of this step: "[We] made a list of all persons we had harmed, and became willing to make amends to them all." This can be a very daunting task unto itself; when doing step four, our searching and moral inventory, in essence this is where this list came from for me; I have found they sort of go hand-in-hand. I found that I added to the inventory when doing this step. The key here is to be thorough, simply because the next step will not go well if you are not, and if you truly wish to get the full effect of doing these steps. When completing this step for the first time, I will say I was very surprised—at myself, mostly—in regards to those people with whom I wanted to make these amends. This also goes back to a person's "perspective" of what is truly being asked of them in this step; it would be degrees of thoroughness needed here if one wants to feel completion.

This is the moment of humility at its finest. Step nine: "[We] made direct amends to such people wherever possible, except when to do so would injure them or others." A tall order, I know, yet the relief I felt in doing these amends was tremendous. I will admit that it took me a fair amount of time, and to be completely honest, I still am not completely finished; but that really is what the point of this entire exercise is. This, for me, is a simple matter of logistics; I was just unable to connect with some of the people I wished to.

This does not mean, however, that I shall just forget about those amends. "Oh well, I tried," just did not seem good enough; I need to put a bit more effort into these people, as when I first put them on "the list." Again, this is a matter of closure, and the utmost importance of that. In my case, as I have already stated, I am not—nor will I ever be—a bad guy, yet the power of the addiction led me to do some very foolish things, in which case I need to own up to them in order for me to move on properly in sound mind.

For me, there is still this one man who I have not made amends to, and that really bothers me every time I think about it. This man in particular was a large part of my getting onto this path, this new journey in the first place. Without his initial persistence of me getting into this program, at a time when I had almost completely given up altogether, I cannot say where I would be today. I *do* know I would not have been able to write this book—this book that I believe can help so many others in their own focus on the entire big picture. We all need a place to start; just as we all had a place where our addictions first took hold without us realizing it, we all have a certain place where our recoveries start, and we are more than likely unaware of this at the beginning. It is not really something that is given priority in these situations.

Step ten is another one where people think *Well, I have done all the hard stuff already, so let's skip it.* I would advise against this: "[We] continued to take a personal inventory and when we were wrong promptly admitted it." This step refers to an ongoing personal inventory we keep for the rest of our lives. To me, this is the only way to interpret these words. At this point in the recovery deal, we should be aware—*very* aware—of, well, self-awareness, among other things that come as a precursor to the self: self-awareness, self-acceptance, self-discovery, self-esteem, self-centeredness, even self-control, self-assurance, sense of self, selfies, self-a-mundo in the immortal words of the Fonz (I thought I needed to lighten up for a moment, forgive me).

This can be an easily discouraging exercise, in that it may seem futile. A good way of looking at this step is just the premise of checking one's self regularly: *Should I be taking this on, or should I be doing this? Is this the right or proper way to handle this situation? Do I, in fact, need to take a step back and possibly think about this a little more before making a rash decision or judgement?* So really—wait for it!—this step is about self-discipline.

"[We] sought through prayer and meditation to improve our conscious contact with God *as we understood Him*, praying only for knowledge of His will for us and the power to carry that out." This would be step eleven. I believe this one is very self-explanatory (more of the self-nonsense eh?), and for the most part, each individual can interpret it as they so see fit. I find this is more of a personal choice as to the meanings set forth, and it will depend on your state of mind at this point in your recovery. Are you a spiritual person or not? Are you not a person that is into prayers at all? It really is up to the individual.

Now, step twelve is a story unto itself in my eyes: "Having had a spiritual awakening as a result of these steps, we tried to carry this message to [addicts], and to practice these principles in all our affairs." Wow—now that's an even *taller* order, don't you think? If, in fact you have had a spiritual awakening, then you do not need to read this next bit for you will already know what your path is going to be (or already is).

Unfortunately, most of us have not had the luxury of this phenomenon; I know I haven't. That is not to say I never will, and again it is really going to be based on your interpretation of what a "spiritual awakening" actually is. This will be different for everyone, and its occurrence will be dependent on many factors. This is not something that one can just force into happening; I really cannot give anymore knowledge on the subject, simply because I just do not know (I'm good, but I'm not that good). Most of this step is truly about helping other addicts who are in the position you once were: People who are looking to become clean and sober yet are so very unsure as to where to turn; people that you perhaps see at a meeting who are new and really don't know of the twelve-step process—that, to me, is the main message of this step. That's another story, though.

So this is my interpretation of the Twelve Steps. The knowledge of myself that I have gained from them—and *continue* to gain on a daily basis—is quite insurmountable. They are something that when you finish them, you don't just toss them away; they become a reference for the rest of your life. Personally, after finishing the first set, I immediately started a second set of steps. There is no reason a person cannot re-do the step work continuously if desired simply because there are so many ways to answer the same questions. Being a perfectionist, this doesn't surprise me, and I am not saying this is for everyone (because it isn't). The fact that the questions are a way of structuring your life is what I'm getting at—they are a way, if you will, to live your life as a clean and sober person. They can be tweaked to match the person's life—*your* life—as long as the initial premise is there. It really is your choice again.

Chapter 8

REALIZATIONS

THIS NEXT chapter is a piece I wrote while in recovery. The reason behind putting this piece in here at this time is simply to show that this is a process that—as one can imagine—is not easy. Many times I would have both fellow clients and the counsellors themselves tell me just how well I was doing in and with the program, and the entire time these were the kinds of things that were going through my mind: I honestly sometimes felt that I would never again be at peace with myself; I had confusion over where I was headed; I didn't know what was next, and how in the hell I was going to get there? It was all just too much. Where do I turn? Someone must have all the answers to the questions I was asking, and I thought it could be found in only one place, that place being within the knowledge of my primary counsellor. The truth is that was just not so.

> There are days when, for some reason, I feel out of sorts. Not sick or ill, just not myself. Some years ago, I apparently suffered from depression, so I am acutely aware of what that particular experience is all about. This time, however, I could not place a finger on what it truly was that was bothering me, so I decided that having been doing this internal work for a good fourteen months now, I knew how to explore this further. Going into this I was very confident that I could come up with some very sound reasoning as to why I was feeling so blasé, so not wanting to talk to anyone, and so ready and willing to isolate myself and figure out the cause of my recent abnormality. Originally, I had the thought that perhaps this was not such a good idea. I brushed this off as nonsense, simply because I felt this is what I have been working towards while dealing with my issues; I've been learning to concisely determine just what it is that is bothering me at any given time, come up with a solution, and be done with it.

Typically, one would think this to be some very sound reasoning, yet I was very wrong on this conclusion. The point of all the talking was just that, to talk—not to isolate oneself in a hole, as I had done in the past. Past indiscretions would most certainly reveal themselves. So why is it that I believed this would work all of a sudden, seemingly out of the blue? For a person to perhaps become or feel they are strong enough to go it alone really does say something about their character—quite possibly the wrong something, but I'll try to explain this the best I know how.

Correct me if I am wrong, but was not the whole purpose of working on one's self with other people to be able to seek out such people when they are what you needed? Is this not exactly what I was trying to learn? Then something miraculous occurred to me—well, maybe not so miraculous. It turned out the reason I was trying to go this alone was because of the person I was seeking out to talk with about these issues. Oddly enough, the issue was nothing either life-threatening or mind-boggling; it really wasn't even anything important. What it was is that I simply had gotten so used to when seeking out this one person was that when I could not find said person, I decided oh well, I can do this on my own because I have learned how to weigh all the pros and cons of a given situation, I've covered all my angles and now I am truly, "good to go." Having thought about this a little longer I understood that my rationale in this was (to say the very least) a bit skewed. Wonky. More likely, it was even somewhat stupid of me to choose this as an avenue to follow, being as fresh out of the gate as I was.

I am not certain that this entire affair is even something that I need to consider, because there is truly nothing wrong; I just don't feel as joyous and happy as I have every day for a good long time now. I have these moments where I will think to myself, *Well, that really sucked*, and that's usually it; it's over and I move on, I forget about it. There are still days from time to time when I think to myself, *Have I in all reality taken myself down the right path this time? I mean sure I'm not drinking anymore, and for the most part, I am generally happy*, yet in retrospect, and surprisingly, I was not unhappy per se when I was drinking. I was emotionally miserable, but not unhappy. I was in relatively good spirits most of the time, simply because the real hurt—and to this day, that is something I do not fully understand, and may never—but that hurt was buried so very deep inside myself that it was as if it was just not there, almost as if the real me had not been present for a very large part of my life.

The thing of it is I have never lived through any emotionally traumatic events of any circumstance—no residential school scenarios, I was not abused as a child in any way, shape, or form, I was raised in such a way to realize right from wrong, and for my growing-up years I was loved as a child (albeit shown this in a roundabout sort of fashion; that was just my family). Honestly, I did not want for anything at all growing up. We—my brothers, sisters, and I that is—may not have had everything that others did, but that was strictly from a disciplinary perspective, from what my father perceived as the best way in which to raise his children. Spoiling the shit out of us was not going to happen on his watch. This is not to say Mom did not from time-to-time if her budget would allow, but where do you think her budget came from? My father; so he was aware, he knew very well, what we did and did not get.

Now, I have to really start to question what is next for me. My treatment is done in a week's time, I move to a new place, I start a new job, I have a new support group for the most part, I am looking for a new counsellor (which I truly wish I did not have to do), I want to continue school to a higher level now, I really want to establish a new career for myself, I have health issues that I have no direct answers to, and all the while my biggest problem right now—the *sole reason* for writing this—is simply that I needed to talk to one certain person about all of these things, and she was not available to do such. It certainly does seem a lot more unimportant now that I have written it all down on paper, yet I could not access the person in question to tell all of my troubles to. Am I just being a big baby? Do I have attachment issues, on top of all my other misgivings? No, I just have preferences, yet I also keep forgetting that one of my issues *on top* of all my issues is that I am centralizing—focusing, if you will—on the fact that I believe this one person in particular is the *only* person who can help me.

When I was unable to talk with her my mood—my feelings, my attitude, my entire processing of normal everyday nonsense—was indescribably shot to hell. So it now comes to my mind again. Addiction can come in the form of anything, and now my addiction seemed to be in the form of another human being. This in itself may sound odd, but I do completely understand it, and it does not surprise me the tiniest little bit. My reliance on my primary counsellor (this, of course, is who I am referring to), was and is so strong, and I know this, but I cannot seem to make any decisions without her input. I know this is inherently wrong. At this point I have turned to others for guidance, yet to me it is just not the same. I was asking others for their support, and for some reason that only increased my need for the acknowledgement of my primary counsellor.

So, seeing this as an "addiction" becomes that much stronger. How can I be addicted to another human being? It really is all in how the situation is perceived; it's not necessarily a bad thing, it really isn't, but everything in moderation, and as an addict, that sometimes is much easier said than done—especially for me, it would seem.

I find the fact that when everything does start going exceptionally well for me, I can still think of ways to destroy these things. It is not self-sabotage because I am aware of what I am doing and I know how to fix these things, *but do I want to?* That is the question. At times, I just get to a place in my head where I just want things to stay as they are, enough with the change already. My God, I have had so much change in my life over the past year that it is truly staggering to think about it all sometimes. Then, of course, I will start comparing myself to others in the same sort of scenario, and I will, God forbid, start to judge. Luckily, I have not done this for a very long time; humility in this instance is a much-wanted and needed perspective. I know the change was necessary for me throughout this last year, and it was the reason why I wasn't seeing the entire big picture, as I do now.

For me, now is the time to start giving back some of that kindness that has been given to me, but also to not forget about those people who are there and are more than willing to help me at the drop of a hat if I am just able to ask. My life cannot revolve around the kind words of strictly one person—something that for me was very difficult to admit in the past.

But this isn't the past anymore. I am a new person, yet the same person I was; my thinking has changed for the better, and I do not wish to return to the past, so I am unsure why I think that way sometimes, but I do know the road to recovery has been long and is by no means over or finished being difficult;

now is definitely not the end of that road for me. The journey has only just begun.

The larger issue here throughout the previous piece was my sole reliance on another person and the fact that I truly did not believe I could sort my problems out for myself; I really did not. To me, it was very bizarre to go back and read this piece six months after penning it. I find it odd that the piece was titled "Realizations," and that I am only at this point coming to this realization. How our minds adapt to the given situations we are faced with on a daily basis is, of course, dependant on our surroundings of the place and time. Just like anything else in life, recovery is determined by this factor, along with so many others, and the loss of one's focus can be overwhelming. The self-realization of our presence of mind—exactly what it is we are doing and saying, and furthermore, trying to accomplish in the present—will take us much further in our future. We have become our own person once again.

Chapter 9

AND HOW THE MIGHTY HAVE FALLEN

Do not let the title deceive you; I do not at all consider myself to be "mighty" by any sense of the word. It is a reference, and only a reference to my precognitive belief that for some inane reason during my addiction years it was just that, the addiction, the booze itself that had led me to believe I was this insurmountable force to be dealt with. I honestly thought that there was nothing I couldn't accomplish with the help of said alcoholic beverages. The simple fact that I got away with it for so very long is indeed a testament to my state of self-worth at the time; in essence, I had none.

Whatever tasks I have taken on in my life I have accomplished and done very well at, no question—that is just a part of my personality. I will not try unless I can do things exceptionally well; otherwise, there was no point. The addiction is what I believed gave me the inner power to do this, to be the best I could be. If that in itself isn't the most fucked up thing you have ever heard, then you are probably still using and really have no use for this book, yet.

Having to start from square one again was anything but easy. I believe I went even further back than this, but really the only further back I could have gone was to the womb. As of yet there has not been a discovery as to how to accomplish this, and to what avail, anyway? Perhaps that's a topic for another book. Anyway, this is a quote, by me, from an earlier writing that holds true here:

> I see a connection in stripping something down to its core—taking its bare bones structure, the parts that are seemingly tried and true—and reinventing them from the ground up.

This is another,

> Of course, this by no means states that I will never again make a stupid

decision. I am almost certain I shall make
many, and strangely I welcome that as
an opportunity, as it is how we grow as
people, as a culture, and as a civilization.

And still another,

What got me to this point in my life was just
that: a culmination of a whole boatload of
stupid and frivolous mistakes, some large
yet most insignificant and compounded over
many years until that boat finally sank. I drove
myself up on the rocks and had nowhere
to go but down, this in itself leading me
to a total re-evaluation of myself from the
absolute lowest common denominator.

Strong words, no?

To be completely honest with myself now was indeed the task I had set upon, and there was absolutely nobody that could deter me from completing this goal. The problem was I no longer had the crutch that I had become so accustomed to for so long to get me through this complicated journey I was about to embark upon. After all, is that not why I was doing this in the first place? The need to overcome the addiction was all-consuming at this point, which meant I truly did have to give up everything I knew—seemingly. This was by far the scariest part for me, the idea of starting all over again. Why had I worked so hard my entire life only to have it all end up in the proverbial toilet I now found myself drowning in? Holy—does that paint a pretty picture, or what?

To say I was at a low point in my life . . . well, yes. The adjective "defeated" had come to what little thinking mind I had left at this particular crossroads of self-exploration. My God, how had I done this to myself? Where in the world was I to even start? Little did I really know what was in front of me now; and I was horrified at the prospects, bleak to say the least, "blind to my tendencies of constant self-doubt concerning not only this decision, but also my entire life, especially now at the present time when this is all new to me from a standpoint of sobriety."

Oddly enough, that last quote was from a piece of writing I did after being sober for sixteen months. It so very perfectly fits my state of mind at the time of my inclusion into the program. The context of each of the statements at their given moments is so utterly different it is frightening, but they give me perspective. It seems that I keep touching on that word, does it not?

So now you may be asking yourself, "Where in the hell are you going with all this?" Here's another quote from a piece of writing I did at fourteen months of sobriety: "I have certainly done some very stupid things throughout my years of addiction, and that was because of the addiction, not because I am a stupid man." See the pattern yet? Does anyone really *ever* change themselves completely? Is this not the point in the book when you should really start to be getting some answers? The problem is, the point of the book is not to give answers at all—those you need to find yourself in your own journey. These are merely ideas I provide, inferences and idioms derived from my own journey that may help. No concrete answers here—sorry.

> Minimizing one's own self-worth is an easy thing to do, in all reality. Having low self-esteem issues is a part of this, and that is not as uncommon as you may think [...] Having the personality type where I question everything I say and do (fully expecting that everyone around me is doing the same thing), and simply believing that nothing I do or did was ever good enough, this of course comes from having low or no self-confidence, which in turn will affect your self-esteem."

Again that quote was from roughly fourteen months sober. Self-worth will also manifest itself in many ways, depending on the make-up of each individual. For me, because of my confidence levels being virtually non-existent, I chose to drink because I believed I became this person that everyone wanted to be around, this person of superior charisma and truly intriguing personality traits. In essence, I was a person so very lonely, living within a huge abundance of people every day, by myself—yeah I know, try and figure that one the hell out, won't you?

I had an incessant need to be the best at everything I did, to be liked by everyone I came in contact with, and to be able to solve the world's problems at seemingly the drop of a hat. People did truly come to me with their problems that were much too extreme for them to cope with and wanted my help, and goddamn it all, I would give them just that. If it was in my power, if it was the least bit feasible, I would do anything—absolutely anything—to help. Can you see how this could become detrimental to my own state of mind? What on God's green earth made me believe I was this all-seeing, all-knowing guru? Perhaps I should have moved to a mountain in Tibet and hired a secretary to take appointments. Holy Moses, I was a *chef* for Christ's sake, what was I thinking? How was this a part of my job description?

Anyway, back to the toilet I was speaking of. At the time I wrote, "I am fully aware that once I start drinking again within a short–*very* short—timeline, I would be in a pine box pushing up daisies. Is this graphic enough?" So now I have to ask myself, yet again, what the hell is my purpose in life anymore? I thought that when I was drinking, at least I was having fun. I *seemed* to be enjoying myself at the time.

That is until the hangover subsided, and I came back to the realization that my life sucked and I was an absolutely miserable individual. I hated my job—if I even had one at the time. I was just waiting for my next EI payment or welfare pittance so I could go and blow it all on booze to once again feel as if everything was going to be okay, simply because I was obliterated yet again. Reality didn't matter until I sobered up, which in turn led me subconsciously to the liquor store over and over until such a time as I was broke—again. At this point I was left with no choice but to face the real world as it is, as well as my regret at my stupidity and self-loathing and shame for having been such an idiot, again.

Yes, the proverbial toilet was beckoning. This was my life now. This was who I had become. I just could not see the forest for the trees. What still bugs the living bejesus out of me to this day was the fact that I was so fully aware of the hell I was putting myself through, and still I refused to do anything about it. What in the name of the Father, the Son, and the Holy Ghost was I trying to prove? Did I honestly think things would just get better all by themselves? Was there a magical alcohol fairy who would supply me with the booze I craved for the rest of my life, so in essence I did not have to think about the harsh reality of that life that seemingly I despised so very much? What planet was I on? Hang on to your knickers—it gets worse.

This is another quote from after sixteen months of sobriety: "I am now, always have been, and forever will be a person of a good heart, a person of relatively sound mind, someone who truly does care about the world around him and the ways in which to help others in any way humanly possible." This is me, and it always has been. Why, then, did I seem to hate myself so much? So it went on and on until such a time as I was evicted—yes, I was now homeless. This is the most horrible conclusion to my now-realized, so very cognizant awareness of what was my life. What crap I had not given away I had put into storage with the last of my money and I was now waiting on a shelter bed—me, the guy who had spent his days in the pursuit of the fruits of life. A guy who was making ridiculously good money at a very young age, and for years and years to follow, I had nothing left, nothing. My daughter hated me, and my ex-wife was extremely pissed at me for having put myself in this predicament; these were the only friends I thought I still had, the only people I thought gave a damn about me anymore—because I sure as shit didn't. People who I thought were my friends mostly bailed out after the money ran out (nice friends, I will say). Was this my rock bottom?

And there I am, waiting for a shelter bed. My goodness, what had I done? My ex-wife had been kind enough to give me some money so I could get a room for a few nights while I waited for this shelter bed, bless her heart; Lord knows she had been given no reason to want to even speak to me, yet she did. Guess what I did? I spent it on booze. Apparently being homeless was just not enough for me to come to the conclusion that I was, in fact, a hopeless alcoholic with a very serious problem. I still could not admit the first step: "[We] admitted that we were powerless over [our addiction]—that our lives had become unmanageable." I had decided I would feel much better with a couple of pints of vodka in me, I would sleep in the park and reassess my situation in the morning, and everything would be okeydokey. What an idiot. Did I mention I was an intelligent man? Where in the hell did that intelligence disappear to on this day? The power of addiction is so very overwhelming. Addicts will put themselves through such stupid shit because, in their own mind, that is the only conceivable alternative, even though it is the worst possible thing they could probably do at that time. It really is frightening, all for the sake of having that "euphoria" that by this point into the addiction is not even present any longer.

Now, you may be asking yourself: why am I reiterating the horror stories of my addiction? I have not really made it a priority of this book until this point, so why now? I do not think the knowledge of my misdeeds is going to help anyone at all, and really, typing all of this is as if I am reliving the entire scenario ... believe me, this has been very unpleasant.

Yet there is a point to all of this. Trust me when I tell you that I really have only touched on some of the main hurdles right at the end of my days of using. This is still a very hard thing for me to talk about in-depth, simply because of the shame of it. I am still a little bit ashamed at and about myself for letting this entire affair go on as long as it did. It hurts, without a doubt.

Things did get worse before they got better. I mentioned my stupidity of using the money for a room to buy booze, then believe it or not, when I did get this shelter bed, of course I assumed I would now be fine; I had a roof over my head and three meals a day for sixty days, now I could figure things out. I got paid and I was going to really get my shit together this time. Guess what I did? I needed to celebrate soooo, you got it, I got drunk yet again and again and again until the sixty days were up and I was again about to be homeless. I assumed I would be able to extend my stay at this shelter. Well, I could have if I wished to sleep on the floor with thirty others. This time, I had no other place to turn—that much I was aware of. Of course, my mind being what it was (or was not because of the addiction), the seriousness had just not sunk in yet. Then the sun went down. It was March; it was raining and very windy as I was wandering downtown Victoria. I was truly at a loss as to where to turn.

I remembered someone mentioning that the Salvation Army will take people in because of the weather, and I really had nothing to lose. I was mere blocks away, so I gave it a shot. Sure enough, the elderly woman at the front reception took pity on me and offered the chapel floor for the night, to my surprise. She told me that if I was sober she would gladly give me a mat and a blanket and pillow and she would leave a message for the caseworker in the morning to see if there were any beds available upstairs. I hadn't even known they had a shelter in the building, but I was grateful and warm once again. Who says minding your manners does not have its benefits? Being sober for the first time in two weeks was also a plus.

It gets worse, believe it or not, and I am still being very tame with this synopsis of my final days on the drink. First, though, my reasoning for this: In my mind, as I stated, listening to horror stories has never helped me in staying sober; if anything, I experienced the exact opposite, hence my lack of interest in the entire AA meeting style. For me going to meetings and listening to others talk about their own awful experiences only depressed me, it made me want to drink to forget the stories I had just heard because it was so relatable to what I was trying to overcome. I failed to see how hearing these stories could be helpful at all and I still do. However, I think it will be very beneficial for me to give you a *glimpse* of just how far down I went before I truly gave in; I had lost absolutely everything, and I still continued on with the addiction. Then I lost even more, and kept on going down like the flush of the proverbial toilet. The further into the addiction I got, the less interest I took in even trying to pull myself out of it, because I thought there was no way in hell I could ever get out of this nightmare; it was so much easier to just drink it away. I had quite honestly given up, and I didn't care any longer.

If nothing else, this chapter is first meant to depress—and then sympathize—with my drama, but the real reasoning for this is to inspire hope, real hope. I could keep going as to how much worse my struggle got before entering the treatment program as I did, but I do not think now it is necessary; you get the idea. I brought myself out of that nightmare with the help of one man's insistence at the program I did enter. Once he got me that bed, it was all up to me.

Well, this is me twenty months later. I'm writing a Goddamn book for shit's sake! Now, that has got to inspire some hope. This is possible, very real and very reachable for those that believe there really is nowhere to turn—I sure didn't have any clue. Once again, I can see a bright future for myself, *without* the crutch that turned into a freakin' ten-tonne weight on my shoulders; not a monkey on my back, baby, but a complete semi-truck and trailer weighing me down.

Writing a book was quite obviously not an easy task—to be sure—but I hope it provides inspiration for others who may be in the same situation that I found myself in. Don't give up; anyone who wants the change can achieve it if they really wish. I am living, breathing proof of that.

If hearing this utter nonsense of what was my life can be of help to just one other person, then the time I have spent writing this will not have been in vain. That is my hope.

Chapter 10

ALTERNATIVES, OPTIONS, AND OTHER AVENUES

At this point, I am again going to clarify some things I have already explained umpteen times in this compendium of all things addiction. To start, I must emphasize again that I am by no means a professional in the field of addiction, but I am an addict—a *recovering* addict, yet still an addict, nothing more, nothing less. I have accepted this as the person I am and have now moved on with the reality that is me. It does not make me (or anyone else, for that matter) any less of a person than the rest of the population of this place we call earth. Because of this little tidbit of reality, I do believe I am qualified to talk about this subject until I am blue in the face. Having said that, my ideas and perspectives—my points of view and feelings of what works and what doesn't—are only my opinions, and have absolutely no guarantee of success whatsoever. That, my friends, is completely up to the individual embarking on this—shall we say—quite possibly life-changing event.

As you are now aware, the route I chose to start my journey of recovery was through the Salvation Army and their addictions treatment facility in the Downtown Eastside of Vancouver. This experience was exactly what I needed for the situation I was in at the time. It is most definitely not for everyone, just as AA is not for everyone. I was in such a place in my head that I truly believed this was the only possibility I had; I was not even sure this would work, to be brutally honest. I really was that far gone. Trying to accomplish sobriety alone at the point of addiction I had evolved myself into would not have worked; I needed the daily structure, I needed to have the accountability as a main focus in my life, and I did not believe anything else would have the slightest bit of a chance in my condition.

I started a daily live-in program where literally my every move was monitored for the first thirty days: then and only then would it lessen, depending on the individual and their circumstances. As I have mentioned, I was one of a very few people in this program who had the option to leave at any time; most others did not. I chose to stay, and believe you me, this in itself was a huge hurdle to overcome. At times, it felt like I was in prison. I bit the bullet and stuck it out, simply because I knew my life could not get any worse than it had already become (with the exception of that pine box I alluded to earlier).

Some of the other things that I had tried in the past—which were numerous—included a group called Life Ring,[7] the Twelve Steps (of course), and another I had invested some time in, referred to as RADAT (Richmond Alcohol and Drug Treatment). There were others still, such as the government-sponsored day programs and workshops. These I would not recommend, but this again is only because of my own poor experience with these programs, and the amount of times I had gone through some of them. Where I was living at the time, these were the only programs available at no cost to me. As I was not working, the options were limited. The entire gamut of the Twelve Step meetings covers any addiction one can imagine; there is a group for that. AA and NA (Narcotics Anonymous) are the most popular

---

[7] *LifeRing Secular Recovery*, http://lifering.org/. Contact them at service@lifering.org.

without question, and they are very successful for an enormous amount of people every day. For me, I was not big on the meetings—and I'm still not. Honestly, I do not remember the last meeting I attended, but that is neither here nor there. They do work; along with the step work they combine to give anyone a sincere and focused sense of direction where this had been lacking in the past for most. I do highly recommend this process for anyone involved in recovery. During my time in treatment the Twelve Steps were a part of my program, and I had little choice but to attend a set amount of meetings every week. Given the choice I now do not, but again, meetings do work for a very great number of people across the world.

Counselling is another avenue I believe to be underrated in its inclusion into one's recovery process. Personally, I still have a private counsellor that I see every two weeks, and shall continue to see her until I deem it unnecessary. It is my choice, and I choose to continue with counselling simply because it helps me a great deal. Even having been sober for seemingly an eternity, I truly feel the counselling I still receive is very necessary in my situation. I still have issues I need to deal with that came to light only after I stopped using my drug of choice; not because I am "crazy," just because I need to able to talk with someone about these issues I have discovered, and for me this is the best way to go about this. I do not have any clue how long I will continue, but I look at it this way: every month, I spend less money on counselling than I used to spend on alcohol, so *you* weigh the odds of which is the better option and let me know which is the better choice. That's the thing; it is a choice, your choice. Again, I would highly recommend the counselling avenue; it is not as scary as people tend to think. One thing one must remember is the fact that you will know on your very first meeting when speaking with a counsellor whether or not they are going to be able to help you in the long-term. That is not to say there are not some really shitty counsellors out there, and you are bound to run into a few of them if you pursue this course. However, do not be discouraged.

As with other people, you are just not going to click with every counsellor you meet. I personally have been through a fair number myself, simply because if I didn't feel the counsellor I was seeing was doing me any good, I would simply stop seeing them and think to myself, *Well, this isn't for me*, and proceed as if there really was nothing wrong in the first place. I would not recommend doing this, either; trust me. Upon first meeting a counsellor, at the end of the session any counsellor worth a grain of salt should ask you what you thought of the session itself—moreover, "What did you gain from this session, and how you feel? Emotionally, was this a good fit? Did you experience any sort of enlightenment during our discussion?"

Okay, I am getting a tad carried away, but the idea here is that if none of this at all happens at the end of a session, then the odds are that that counsellor is not going to do you any good. Find another, and do not waste your time. Ask the counsellor you were talking with to recommend someone else, because you did not feel a connection. And again, any counsellor worth their hard-earned credentials will NOT have any problem giving you a reference. Unless, of course, you are an ass about it—so don't do that either. I cannot say enough about the benefits I have received from this line of self-discovery. It has helped me in so many ways, that I have truly lost count.

Be persistent in your search. It may take some time to find a counsellor that you can "click" with, but in the long run, the benefits are exponential.

There is another option that many people also overlook. This could be for many reasons, but I think the biggest one is because it is right in front of most people and they are just too afraid to ask. This option would be your family. If you are in the position of having a family with whom you are close, then seek them out in these circumstances. I realize these are situations that are not always possible, usually because of the addiction and its length and severity. However, if the opportunity is present, then grasp onto it; you may be very surprised at how easily an estranged or even disillusioned family member will come around when they realize that you are serious about this—unless, of course, you are not; then don't waste their time with your nonsense.

I still have a father that really has no clue what my addiction has entailed. He believed that once I stopped drinking that I would magically become this wonderful person; he thought all of my problems had stemmed from the booze. So with that taken out of the equation, he believed I was a fine, upstanding citizen again. The thing he *didn't* understand is I have always been a fine, upstanding citizen, booze or not. I was just an alcoholic. When I tell him I am *still* an alcoholic he questions me: "Well how can that be if you no longer drink?" He just doesn't get it, and he probably never will. So be it; he doesn't have to live with the reality of being a recovering alcoholic.

Remember that daughter I mentioned who wanted nothing to do with her daddy? Guess what? She is now one of my greatest supports. Throughout the treatment program there were many times that I was, let's say, a wee bit depressed. At the time I just didn't see why or how I could bring myself out of the pit of despair I found myself in. Sure, I was sober, but I was also so unhappy with virtually *everything* and I had nowhere to turn—or so I thought. It didn't seem to matter what time of day or night it was; she was willing to talk. Let's just say I was very pleasantly surprised by this, as I certainly had given her no reason to want to help. The amount of events I had missed during her growing years is ridiculous, not because

I didn't want to be at these events, but because the power of the addiction was stronger than my desires to see her. This is one of the things I still harbour some shame about, but she has forgiven me. Jesus, I missed her graduation for Christ's sake. That must not have been an easy thing to forgive, but she has.

Her mother has also been there for me throughout this entire sordid affair. Although this does not shock me, we were almost married once. We remained close after we broke up, simply because we did have a daughter together. Well, it really isn't quite that simple. Suffice it to say, she has never given up on me; she has always known in her mind that I was capable of this whole sobriety thing, and even though there have been some very extensive disagreements throughout this, she has stuck by me in ways that have baffled me to no end. I certainly didn't give her any reason to continue her escapade of seemingly fruitless efforts to help me.

There really are so many things I could say here regarding her persistence, her truly amazing character; her ability to forgive is sometimes astonishing. Did I mention she is a recovering alcoholic herself? That may have something to do with her persistence, but the thing is one of her greatest supports is now and always has been her family. I could never understand how this was even remotely possible until I was sober myself, and now I do. Her family has always been very close, whereas I am not terribly close with mine. I really didn't know what the value of this connection was. Even when we all still lived under the same roof, my family has been estranged from each other; odd, I know, but we are a funny bunch as families go. We more or less tolerated each other, but I don't know if I could ever call us close, except that we are "family." If my brothers and sisters ever read this, I am sure I will get some mixed reactions about that comment. Good, bad, or indifferent—they are still your family.

I have four siblings in my family, and one of the last places I ever thought I could turn in this situation was to them. All reasoning aside I just didn't think there was anything there to turn to. Again, I was pleasantly surprised. My little sister, who I never would have thought could have been of any support whatsoever, has been amazing throughout my recovery. Hell, she even knitted me some mittens! Again, any time I needed to talk she was there, day or night, with a kind word or some sound advice, or a point of view I had not even considered. Keep in mind she lives on the other side of the country, and we have not seen each in God knows how long; thirty years, if my memory is correct, yet she is there for me.

It's funny, because again, we were not terribly close, but at the same time we were. My little sister and I fought like cats and dogs usually, but we did see eye-to-eye, whatever the hell that actually means. She is still a phenomenal support throughout my recovery; she understands the whole process of loss, anger, grief, desire, and, well, *addiction*. She understands addiction. Being an intelligent woman, she has knowledge as an outsider from addiction. She is not an addict, but has been exposed to addiction in her own life. My other sister has also been supportive, but to say she understands in the same way would not be correct. It is a difficult thing to understand with an unbiased view—believe me. What I am saying here is to never discount anyone in this ordeal, especially family. Because of that bond we share as a family, there is nothing else like it, so if given the chance to grasp it, do it.

The Twelve Step programs can also be a large part of anyone's successful recovery process. They are still a part of mine—just not to the extent they once were. I am still doing a set of steps. When I finished the first set of steps that I looked deeper into in Chapter 7, I did not feel as if I was done. So I started a second set, this time using the AA step work versus NA, which I had done for the first set. They are very similar in the outlook as they are all derived from the exact same premise; they are simply more specified to the addiction which you are dealing with. Being an alcoholic, I did not feel I was finished with the step work until I specifically did a set of AA steps. That's just me, and I will probably do a third and a fourth and a fifth etc. set of steps until the day I no longer walk this earth. This is not an uncommon occurrence. In all reality, this is a grounding of sorts, a point of origin to which one can return over and over for a fresh start, if needed.

As I stated in Chapter 7, this is an opportunity to be as brutally honest with yourself as humanly possible. Otherwise, there really is no point in doing the steps. Personally, being a perfectionist, I may never believe I am finished doing the step work, but what can it hurt to want to constantly reassess oneself, within reason, of course? So what is it that I am leading up to here? You may have noticed I have used the word "support" over and over again. Trust me: this is not because I have run out of alternatives; the *support* network that one has during, after, and forever is by far the most important part of this entire process. It's so important that I have dedicated an entire chapter to this in itself, and one can never ever, ever, ever, ever, have enough support. Trust me on this one; I have tried so many times to go this alone, and it just doesn't work out so well, ever. Maybe for a while, but long- term is what we are talking about, and our support network is going to change, just as our friend's change. The constant here is to have the support, just the support.

Funnily enough, you can find support in almost any place you desire, with almost any person you wish, if you are simply upfront about it. By this I do not mean one has to profess their addiction to the masses, not by any stretch of the imagination. As with the rest of the recovery process, one of the keys is to just be as gut-wrenchingly honest as you can possibly be. This is going to scare some people away, but you know what? There are billions of people on this big round ball we call Earth. Look around; you'll find someone else, and then another and another. I guarantee this.

Chapter 11

I SHOULD HAVE ...

Throughout the course of their lives, who has not done something they have regretted? Who has believed that they are accomplishing something extraordinary, only to have it blow up in their face? Who has found out that what they have done was the stupidest thing they could have ever *considered* doing in the first place? Trust me; I've been there. "How foolish can a person be" is the question that comes to my mind, but perhaps you honestly thought you were taking the best course of action.

Anyway, throughout my sordid affairs, my addiction, and then during my initial recovery process, I found that I was making some really stupid mistakes of an incredible magnitude. No, really; it wasn't that bad. Moreover, these were a few things that I noticed about myself that I was doing, but not yet realizing the harm these things could incite if given the chance. What really is the point of telling yourself I should have done this or I should have done that? How will this be helpful now? These are only a few of the idiosyncrasies that I realized about myself in my recovery. There are many more that I did not experience that just seem as if they are a part of one's everyday existence. Alas, they are not. Be careful, as things have a tendency of sneaking up and biting one on the ass. This is not recommended. The last thing you need—during the initial recovery, especially—is things you, well, *do not need*. I am not sure how else to explain this phenomenon.

This book is about addiction and to say that we as a whole are "graced" with having addictive personalities would be a gentle way to put it. As I mentioned in an earlier chapter—Chapter 8, if I am not mistaken—I truly believed I was addicted to another human being. Although this is a bad analogy of what I am referring to, it fits the purpose nicely here. The amount of recovering addicts that just seem to shift their drug of choice to another substance—not necessarily another hallucinogenic substance, either—is where the difficulty in comprehending this phenomenon appears. Being clean and sober ... hmmm, have you happened to notice that if you were a coffee drinker, you are now drinking a whole shitload more coffee than you used to? Huh? If in fact you were a drinker such as myself, have you noticed the dramatic increase in your sugar intake of late? I did not, until such a time as I had gained fifty pounds (well, forty-eight, in a relatively short period of time). I personally have never had an issue with my weight, yet the gut I possessed for a short time was surprising, to say the least. Think about it for a minute, how much sugar, natural or not, is there in alcohol? Let me tell you; there is a whole hell of a lot, so naturally the body is going to crave that substance. It doesn't care if it comes distilled or not; your body does not know the difference. Your brain knows the difference of the effects of the alcohol versus that of the sugar and it will compensate—but this is what I am talking about, substituting one "narcotic" for another. Alcohol or sugar: yes, they have very different effects, but in essence they are accomplishing the same thing in your brain, believe it or not.

I am not about to get into the logistics of brain function at this point, so if in fact that is what you were hoping for, well forget it. A brain guy I am not, with the exception of the fact that when sober I am of above-average intelligence. I had forgotten this. I only know the things I have experienced during my own recovery, and this does not mean this is what everyone else on the face of the planet is going to go through. Again, how is it that I believed I was addicted to another person? I was not; this is referred to as "transference," and I will try and explain this as best I know how.

What I had done was taken the professional relationship with my counsellor and turned it into one of affection—affection that wasn't actually there, only in my mind. I had been in a place of seclusion for so long because of the drink and my addiction, and this was the first person who had shown me any semblance of care in a very long time. I took this concern for me as something it was not. Do not misunderstand me; she cared about my well-being, as this is a huge part of the profession she has chosen to dedicate her life, but not in the way that I was interpreting it. I, of course, realized this, and we shared our feelings and everything was copacetic and we moved on with the counselling as if nothing had occurred. Had we not done this, the possibility of our client/counsellor relationship could very easily have come to an end simply because of professional ethics and the parameters involved with such. What I had done in my mind was I had replaced my alcohol addiction with another human being. I assumed that if another person cared about me that my life would magically become this wonderful place. The problem is that if we are not able to overcome our issues by ourselves, then we will never truly be healed. We are working on our deepest, darkest misgivings of ourselves, and no one knows us better than us. Strange as that may sound, it is reality. The idea is to find the tools you need to be able to proceed with your recovery by yourself—with the help of a support network, yes—but the key is to become once again self-sufficient in every way, shape, and form.

Imagine, if you will, another place and time. No seriously, imagine entering into a personal relationship while still in the recovery process. What in all honesty do you think is going to come about from this rather intrepid endeavour? Here's another question: how many relationships break up because of addiction? So to be blatantly honest, do you really think that starting a relationship while still in the early stages (or even the later stages) of recovery is the best idea? Probably not, right? I have seen so many people throughout my recovery who seem to think this is the only way they will get through this thing, and I can tell you with a whole lot of certainty that this is, in more cases than not, not going to end well. Many relationships where one or both people are addicts are going to be strained, without a doubt, and quite a good number of them are never going to be the same again. Also, in my experience, they do not last, especially if only one party decides to get clean in the relationship while the other is still using. This never ends well.

There really is no way that one, with 100% certainty, can focus on oneself if there is another person in that scenario; it is, at the very least, extremely difficult. You can give it a shot, and I wish you luck, but I would not hold my breath. The ability to focus on yourself while in a relationship is difficult, simply because of the relationship itself. Where is your main focus going to be if you are in a relationship? Typically, if it is a caring relationship, your thoughts will be on the significant other more than oneself, no? That has been my experience anyway, and that's not to say I am not unique in every thing I do—I am. The point is, where is your main focus—yourself, or your partner? Where should that focus be—yourself, or your partner? Is the relationship deterring you from doing the things you need to do in order to build that support network that you will need to stay clean and sober for the rest of your life? *Focus.* Are you more worried about who's going to walk the dog? Who's going to scoop the litter box? Focus—where is your focus? Do you see where I'm going with this? Have I made my point? Are you listenin' to the words that are comin' outta my mouth?

As wonderful as relationships can be, in this instance they can become very harmful to the final outcome of what is trying to be accomplished here; it's just the way it is, I am sorry to say. Get yourself clean and sober for a good long while, and *then* if that significant other really was just that, they will still be there. That's when you will realize you really were in a quality relationship in the first place. There are exceptions to this, sure, but that is not for me to decide. Again, this is from my experiences, and it is based off what does not/has not worked for me, or the many others I have seen fail because of this.

The phrase "ticking time bomb" just popped into my head. Be prepared, because throughout the recovery process, our thinking will change in many ways. If in fact you *are* in a relationship, one may expect that is going to also change. Companionship is a wonderful thing, but is it really helpful through this, or will it be a deterrent? These are all things that need to be considered. Understand that yes, the relationship is a form of support absolutely, but is it the kind of support that is needed? Again, this is a judgement call that needs to be made by the individual dependent upon the circumstances present at the time of the life-altering event that is about to be undertaken. I know I am getting somewhat dramatic, but it is food for thought. What is it that you truly wish to accomplish here: healing yourself *for* yourself, or are you doing this for someone else? Think about it . . .

I have to say, that last spiel exhausted me, even just re-reading it. However, it really is something that requires a fair amount of thought as to where the priorities lie in your life. This is not to say you need to start over completely—and I believe I have covered that in previous chapters very thoroughly–but this is important, which is the reason why I'm harping on about this issue.

My reasoning for titling this chapter as I have is because of the need to understand that what you could have done differently in the past is really of no concern to you now. What's done is done, and it is the time to move forward; the reasoning behind the step work is so all of these past indiscretions can be dealt with in as timely a fashion as possible. Depending on the content of the eighth and ninth steps, this is where you will receive the most amount of closure on things that you now cannot change, even if you wanted to. The past is the past, so leave it in the past, especially when you are still dealing with the underlying issues. I did *not* say forget about the past, no—just leave the past in its place, in the grand scheme of things. The past still matters—in some cases a great deal—yet usually it is something we should file away until needed.

Oddly, I personally had a piece of my past slap me across the back of the skull just the other day, and now I have to deal with this issue in order to proceed with my journey. This is after I thought I was done with all the amends and all-encompassing forgiveness and apologies and the like. See what I mean? The past does not go away, even if you try to make it do so. If it doesn't need to be your main focus, then file it away. Trust me; when it needs you, and this will usually occur at the most inopportune time, your past will inevitably find you. When it does, what you should have done will again become relevant—but not really. So you see, it doesn't matter; now is the time to deal with the issue at hand, and not what you should have or would have done in the past. As confusing as this sounds it really isn't.

Just as in normal life—although our lives do now seem anything but normal—shit does still happen. Hopefully, we are now strong enough within our personal headspaces that we are able to deal with these situations as they come—and they will abound, at times—and we have the knowledge and the courage to understand and proceed within the parameters of life, without returning to the comfort of the addiction for solace or to just plain hide from that life as we have done so very many times in the past. Look where that led us, right?

Chapter 12

DAYS OF WINE AND ROSES

You may wonder why in the name of all that is holy that I chose such a title for the conclusion—or for any part of this book. One would think this could be a sign of self-destruction, wouldn't one? Ah, but there is a method to my madness; truly, I wish I could take credit for that line, yet I digress.

My life as such has been many things over the rather illustrious fifty years of my existence. I have seen and done so many unique things within and around my chosen career. I have met many famous (and not so famous) people; even a few infamous folks that I would much rather forget all about, thank you very much. Through it all there really is no other part of my life that can compare to what it really is that I possess now. I could say that now, being of sound mind (and almost of body), the booze did take its toll over the years. It's nothing that is about to kill me in the very near future, in case you were worried. But you know what? That's not it, that's not it at all.

I do have to admit that there are things from my past days of addiction that I can no longer do that I dearly miss sometimes. A really huge one for me being an alcoholic was going out for an exceptional dinner with a friend and being able to pair each course of the meal with a fine wine. This I truly miss, as it was never about the addiction, but just being a former alcoholic it is a particular pleasure that I know I will never again be able to enjoy. This is very unfortunate to someone with a palette such as mine; you need to be either a chef or a wine connoisseur to truly appreciate this sense of pleasure, this sense of contentment—trust me. But again, this will never again be a part of my life. I will have to look at it through the eyes of a person who has already had these fine experiences, and just leave it as a memory of such things in the future. I believe I can do this.

There's another thing I will miss (yet I know there are many ways other than this particular way to reward oneself after a gruelling workday). I am speaking about the end of the shift, after a hot and sweaty day, when nothing is finer than an ice-cold beer. There really is no comparison; for me, however, it will have to be lemonade from this point on. *C'est la vie mon amie.*

There are many such things that I took great pleasure in that I will no longer be able to enjoy; it seems the majority are related to the hospitality industry, unsurprisingly, since that has been my career throughout the greater portion of my adult life. I remember the wine tastings that I used to host at this one particular restaurant chain, with which I did the majority of my culinary training. Wine tasting is an extremely valuable tool to possess in this industry (although it may not be openly apparent to the average individual). It is vital to have a combined knowledge of the wines themselves and the food pairings that I am also preparing—whether it is an accompaniment, or a base for a mouth-watering sauce for a prime cut of beef or the freshest bounty from the seas. It's all relative, and it doesn't mean I cannot still cook with fine wines and ridiculously expensive cognac, pernod, aquavit, apple brandy, or even masala—it just will not be the same! Seriously, one must share both my love of food—cooking the finest cuisine on earth—combined with the best spirits of the world to understand. I am not referring to the ghosts in the attic, either; I will not be able to indulge, and you know what? Sure, I'll miss this, but

I'll get by—I really will. I'm guessing my reference in the title of this chapter is starting to make a tad more sense now. Could anyone ever have guessed I was a recovering alcoholic with all the talk of the booze?

In many respects, I think a main point I am trying to get across here is that life does not have to become a mixed bag of boredom simply because the drug of choice has now been removed. It really doesn't. I will also miss the parties, but in retrospect, how many bloody times did I make a complete ass of myself at said parties, simply from imbibing just a wee, teeny-tiny bit too much? Absolutely; they were fun—I had fun, I think, from what the hell I can remember, anyway. Usually only the finer points of my own stupidity have been related back to me after all was said and done. Believe me, most of these stories I would much sooner forget, but you get the idea. Now I can go to these parties—if I ever again even choose to—and be able to remember them; that in itself is a novel concept, don't you think? Having fun for the sake of having fun, and not having what I perceive as fun after ten or twenty wallops of whiskey, and then having ten or twenty people tell me the next day after sleeping off the hangover how much "fun" I really did have because I simply cannot remember all that glorious fun I was a part of (the centre of) because of all that glorious, free-flowing whiskey that had been my best friend the previous evening. Sounds like a real hoot, right? Oh, the stories of my stupidity I could tell you, yet again, I digress. If in fact you have not seen the point of all of this yet, then quite possibly you are not ready to live a clean and sober life. Think about it, though: you have made it this far in this reference guide to recovery, so if you have not made a decision yet, then maybe it is the time to.

To truly describe my state of mind now is a very monumental task, because in many respects I do not yet understand it all myself, and I may never. That's the beauty of it, I think: I am happy. Honestly, I cannot remember the last time I was able to say this. Really. So in itself, that really is a mouthful. So many things that in the past would have just sloughed off as pure nonsense because I was so unhappy are now absolutely precious to me. A few days ago, a woman who I really do not know all that well told me that I should be proud of myself for all of the work I have done to improve myself during my time in the recovery program, where I am now an employee. She said to me that I am an inspiration to others coming into and going through the same program. Holy, I know, right? Those words were truly foreign to me; I mean sure, I have been recognized for my work in the professional stance simply because I am very good at what I do. To me, it was just a no-brainer to be recognized for such. It was expected, and I wrote it off as nothing; it meant nothing to me, simply because I didn't ever see the value in it before. My perspective on the entire subject of one's self-worth is completely altered from what it once was.

The next day, I saw another woman who had been one of my counsellors and is now a friend and a part of my ongoing support network. Well, I made her cry! You know what? I was very proud of myself for being able to do this, for having the ability to make a person cry with mere words. Goddamn, I was freakin' elated with myself...

Perhaps I got a little too excited there, my apologies, let me explain. If you will go back to the acknowledgements of the book itself, her name is mentioned as one of three amazing professionals and all-around good people that helped me throughout this entire process of mine. She read the dedication and she was brought to tears, and then when she tried to explain to me how that dedication made her feel, she was in tears again. Cool, huh? Of course, when I tried to explain I myself, was also in tears, just as I was when I wrote it, so quite obviously these are tears of joy and not sadness, which is all I used to know. For many, crying derives from despair, but that is not always the case. I said to her that the words I typed are simply the way I feel; I cannot change that, and I am not willing to hide the way I feel any longer. I want to *feel* things—good, bad, or indifferent, it really doesn't matter. Simply the act of feeling is an ongoing growth process that I shall continue to do for the rest of my life now.

That I have been able to touch another person in such a way simply by being myself is a feeling that has to be experienced to be fully understood. It is a nice way to feel, I guarantee this. If I could do this every single day for the rest of my life to someone new, I would be a very happy man indeed. It's a nice way to approach this big, bad, cold world of which we are a part. Why would anyone not want to feel this? Now that I can see this, now that I can now feel these things, would I ever want to go back to the life of my past? Why in the hell would anyone? And you know what? It is not as if I have experienced this great epiphany because, I have not; I simply have learned to appreciate the finer things in life. That has nothing to do with being rich, owning a yacht or a mansion, driving an Aston Martin, or having twenty servants at your every beck and call. It would be nice, but a happy person it does not make.

I, my friends, am happy.

I am assuming that people would be wondering just what it is that makes me so happy? Really, I guess the thing of it is a person's own mind; how does an individual come to the conclusion that they are indeed happy? I did not just get up one morning and discovered I was miraculously a completely different human being; my work within the recovery program was nothing miraculous, per se. My persistence at this was very thorough, yes, but I cannot say it's *complete*, as I do not believe it ever will be. This is a lifelong process. There is always something more that can be done, and we can never forget that.

The time that I invested both within and outside of the facility's walls was significant; this should be a no-brainer, but it is not. There were definitely times where I wanted to have nothing to do with anybody; I truly wanted to just be left alone, and for everyone and everything to go away and leave me to my own devices. Realizing those "devices" had not worked so very well for me in the past, I knew this was not the proper way to go about things. It was very hard, no doubt about that, and some days it still is. I was intensely aware that I could not shut off the outside world as I had done when I first arrived at the treatment centre. I did not want to; moreover, I was terrified to go out the doors for fear of where I would end up. I knew I could not stay here in the protective bubble I had created for myself for the rest of my life; one day, I would have to untie the apron strings and return to the real world. No lie—this scared the living daylights out of me. One of the reasons I stayed as long as I did was because I was terrified that I would leave and not have the support I needed to continue with this recovery myself, something I had done in the past (and quite obviously failed). Realizing I had this now is what gave me the courage to leave. Trust me, I didn't want to stay as long as I did, yet I knew I needed to, I knew I was not ready. There was no shame in this. I was just not ready, I knew it, and nobody was pushing me out the door, just the opposite, which to me was extremely comforting during that time of uncertainty. There, I had the support I needed and I felt safe; leaving, I did not.

I have always been of a mindset that I never walk into anything blind. I am always fully aware of what I am getting myself into, or I won't proceed. I have always done my research and followed through secure in the knowledge I was prepared in everything I have done—strangely, even my addiction. Yes, when I went out to use, I made sure I could get what I wanted, nothing less. During my addiction, if I felt I did not have enough money to buy enough booze to get as destroyed as I wanted to, then I would not drink. Really, how ridiculously insane is that line of thought? Yet I did this over and over again, as this was the rationale of my mind at the time.

So why I am happy? I am fifty years old now, and I am just finishing my grade twelve education. I am in college again. I am working a full-time job. I have people in my life who truly care about my well-being, and not just the people who were getting paid to care, as when I was in the program. As cold as that may sound, that is the reality of it. I have friends again; something that was unknowingly non-existent for a very long time, with the exception of a few that have stuck by me through this entire ordeal. My beautiful child actually wants her daddy in her life. My sisters are genuinely concerned for my continued recovery.

Even my father sort of understands, and trust me, that is saying a lot, that is another book altogether. Even my daughter's mother, shall I dare to say, worries. I will more than likely be reprimanded for that last line, but you know what, that's okay too. She never gave up on me; she threatened to many times, and I will never understand the reasoning behind her persistence in wanting me to succeed, yet I'm sure as hell glad she stuck it out. I do not think I would be where I am if that persistence, compassion, and yes love for another person was not present. Are you still unsure as to why I am happy?

My life is not the thing that dreams are made of, by any stretch of the imagination. I am not rich. I do not have supermodel girlfriends, I do not drive an AC Cobra, hell I don't even have a licence. I do not have a private jet or a mansion or a bank account that contains the riches of the world. I don't even have a cat or a plant for that matter. What I have are the things that matter to me, the little things that most people truly take for granted. I can watch a beautiful sunset or enjoy a compelling conversation—or even a ridiculously stupid one—and remember them. I can listen to a purely innocent repertoire between a father and his daughter and just be present in the moment, simply because it reminds me of precious memories I have of my own child. Life is hard sometimes, but it really doesn't have to be. As much as it terrified me for so very long, living as a clean and sober individual is a very rewarding experience that, for me, can only get richer and fuller every day.

Just think: a published author. That's pretty interesting, no? I guess if you have read this book, that last line has come to fruition. I have accomplished another of the many tasks I had set out for myself before I was so blatantly interrupted by a bottle screaming my name, over and over again. This is a journey that I shall continue to relish with open arms for as long as the man upstairs sees fit. And I'm just fine with that.

Bibliography

Alcoholics Anonymous. *The Big Book*. 4th ed. Alcoholics Anonymous World Services, 2001.

Alcoholics Anonymous. *Twelve Steps and Twelve Traditions*. New York: Alcoholics Anonymous World Services, 2001.

Barber, Katherine, Heather Fitzgerald, Tom Howell, and Robert Pontisso. *Oxford Canadian Dictionary of Current English*. Don Mills, ON: Oxford University Press, 2005.

Resources

The Salvation Army

Founded: 1865, in the East End of London, England

Headquarters: London, United Kingdom

Founders: William and Catherine Booth

Subsidiaries: Salvation Army Vision Network, The Salvation Army Evangeline Booth College, and Reliance Bank

LifeRing Secular Recovery

LifeRing Service Center

1440 Broadway, Suite 400

Oakland, California, 94612

service@lifering.org

The Salvation Army Harbour Light Addiction Recovery and Rehabilitation Centre

119 East Hastings Street

Vancouver, British Columbia, V6A 1K8

About The Author

J.P. WILLSON is a writer and chef living on the west coast of Canada. Growing up as the shy, quiet child in a large middle-class family, he has always been an observer, a thinker, and a wonderer. He has worked as a Red Seal chef for twenty-five years, and is highly skilled in his trade. However, despite his accomplishments, his life has not been easy. J.P. struggled with alcoholism for nearly thirty years, which resulted in homelessness, unemployment, loneliness, and spiralling depression. Having done the soul-searching and continuing work required for recovery, J.P. decided to share his experience and knowledge to help others along their own journeys. *Through the Mind's Eye: A Journey of Self-Discovery* is his first publication. J.P. is deeply grateful for the love and support of his family, counsellors, and friends.

CPSIA information can be obtained
at www.ICGtesting.com
Printed in the USA
LVHW090814051219
639473LV00001B/2/P